Brahms

Brahms

Hans A Neunzig

translated by Mike Mitchell
introduced by Peter Sheppard Skærved

HAUS PUBLISHING · LONDON

Originally published in German under the title JOHANNES BRAHMS in the
Rowohlt monographien series
Copyright © 1973 Rowohlt Taschenbuch Verlag GmbH, Reinbek bei Hamburg

The English translation first published in Great Britain in 2003 by
Haus Publishing Limited
32 Store Street
London WC1E 7BS

A CIP catalogue record for this book is available from the British Library

ISBN 1-904341-17-9 (paperback)

Typeset in Garamond at Palimpsest Book Production Limited, Polmont,
Stirlingshire

Printed and bound by Graphicom in Vicenza, Italy

Front cover: painting of Johannes Brahms
courtesy of the Lebrecht Music Collection
Back cover: photograph courtesy of the Lebrecht Music Collection

CONTENTS

Introduction

For many young musicians, the first powerful encounter with
Johannes Brahms will not be through his music, but through his
image; and the image they will often first encounter is Willy von
Beckerath's famous drawing of the composer at the piano. Brahms
is pictured sitting in profile, his feet close together on the pedals,
his Mosaic beard hanging down over his protruding belly. Leaning
back from the piano, a cigar clamped between his teeth, he appears
to be playing a deeply articulated
chord, such as the opening notes
of the first violin-piano sonata
which he wrote for Joseph Joachim,
the G major Op 78, sometimes
named for the song it incorpo-
rates, *Regenlied*.

Eugenie Schumann describes
his playing in her memoirs: 'We
would often sit talking at the
breakfast table for a long time, but
Marie reminded him sometimes,
"Herr Brahms, you really must
practise now, or you will not play
properly at the concert." Then he

Brahms at the piano. Willy von
Beckerath, 1899

always got up obediently, went into the music room with his
beloved cigar, and presently we heard the vigorous attack of his
two fifth fingers, one at each extreme end of the keyboard, and
arpeggios in counter movement through endless modulations followed. Interesting as this playing was, there was always something of a fight or animosity about it. I do not believe that

Brahms looked upon the piano as a dear trusted friend, as my mother did, but considered it a necessary evil, which one must put up with as best one could.'[1]

But the most wonderful thing about Beckerath's portrait is the expression on Brahms's face. With his eyes closed and his features rapt, this overweight, prematurely ageing, tweedy, silver-bearded man looks like an angel, or Coleridge's vision of the poet: 'Beware, beware, his shining eyes, his waving hair.'[2] Every time I remember this print, it brings to mind Robert Schumann's ecstatic note after meeting him for the first time:

'I think that if I were younger I could make some polymetres about the young eagle who has so suddenly and unexpectedly flown down from the Alps to Düsseldorf. Or one might compare him to a splendid stream which, like Niagara, is at its finest when precipitating itself from the heights as a roaring waterfall, met on the shore by the fluttering of butterflies and nightingales' voices . . . The young eagle seems to be content in the lowlands; he has found an old guardian who is accustomed to watch such young flights, and who knows how to calm the wild wingflapping without detriment to the soaring power.' While to Joseph Joachim, the great Hungarian violinist who had introduced Brahms to Schumann, he simply penned: 'This is he that should come.'[3]

Brahms himself would probably have preferred the image presented in Beckerath's portrait to Schumann's description, for image control was of the greatest importance to him. Indeed there was never a more efficient self-censor than Johannes Brahms. He seems to have been constantly making bonfires of his sketches, juvenilia and letters, destroying everything that might fuel controversy about his interpretation or compositional integrity; and perhaps more importantly, immolating any documents that might reveal hairline cracks in the adamantine flawlessness of his carefully modelled, self-made image, before or after his death.

Curiously, he seems to have been most worried that subsequent generations would discover how little preparatory sketching he did before going to work on the actual manuscript of a new piece. He seems to have felt that he would not come off particularly well if his meagre sketching were ever to be compared to Beethoven's monumental researches prior to composition. Thus, Brahms was his own literary executor, press agent and 'Ministry of Truth', all rolled into one, and he continued to burn his personal papers right up until the end of his life.

From the viewpoint of an inquisitive performer, the result of all of this is infuriating. Mozart, Beethoven and Schubert's manuscripts are proof of the process of their composing. They show where the composers changed their minds, and where they rewrote passages in collaboration with colleagues, be they performers or other composers. There are even little reminder notes about paying creditors, and records noting the arrival of unwelcome visitors. Elgar tended to draw fantastic animals on his pages when he was bored, or to write encouraging or disparaging notes to himself. These scores are all clear manifestations of the act of composing, and have provided fuel for speculation for generations of scholars and performers. By contrast, most of Brahms's surviving manuscripts are *Rheinschriften*, or fair copies, made as exemplars of a notion of 'pure' composition, which Brahms became ever keener to create and protect as he grew older.

In 1996, a Brahms treasure appeared for sale at Sotheby's in London. This was the manuscript of his two late sonatas for piano with clarinet, perhaps the two greatest sonatas written for that instrument, and the jewels of the flowering of his late chamber music. The pieces were written for and dedicated to the clarinettist and violinist Richard Mühlfeld – *Hrn. Richard Mühlfeld Dem Meister seines schones Instrumentes, in freundlich dankbarer Erinnerung! J. Brahms, Ischl im Sommer '95*[4] – and the manuscript had remained in the possession of the Mühlfeld family ever since. It is perhaps the single most important Brahms relic ever to appear at auction, for the manuscript of these two late sonatas is far from being a fair copy.

The beautifully bound folio, 44 pages in length, is embossed with the words *'"Manuscripte von Brahms", Ischl 1894'* in large, fading gold leaf letters on the tooled red leather cover, and upon opening, it yields up an extraordinary surprise. Instead of the elegant, copybook musical handwriting of the well-known Brahms, such as that seen on the score of the Op 79 piano *Rhapsodies*, or on the clean manuscript of the Violin Concerto Op 77, which is littered with Joseph Joachim's emendations in shockingly bold red ink, this is a working text. The score is heavily over-written, with countless scratchings and crossings-out. There are extensive revisions, deleted sections, alterations and corrections to both the parts. Many passages are rewritten on separate pages and free staves, and indicated with cues, including some written on slips of manuscript paper pasted in the margins, along with remarks to the music copyist. Themes are jumbled up with their possible alternatives, and messy indications of possible transpositions float like ghosts over the ink text.

It is a chaotic looking score, more closely resembling the creative jumble of Charles Ives's (1874–1954) four polystylistic Violin Sonatas (1906–12), which were begun around a decade after Brahms penned his Clarinet Sonatas Op 120, than anything we are accustomed to from Brahms. It is a surprising comparison to find oneself making. One expects to see Ives's mess, his collaging and cut and paste techniques; it's germane to any understanding of his music. 'Herr Doktor' Brahms's carefully preened musical image, however, and, by extension, our understanding of his working methods, runs completely counter to the muddled revelation of these scores. For the score of the two sonatas reveals many 'proto-Ivesean' techniques at work. Sections of the music have been physically cut from one part of the score and pasted over others, and drastic elisions have been made without any attempt to rationalize the linear anomalies that ensue. Brahms was attacking his own constructional integrity in order to maximize the dramatic effect of the music, working like a great film editor turning a rambling epic into a concise, powerful three-act drama.

The surprising reality of this score can only lead to speculation that much of the apparently Spartan, succinct quality of these late works has more to do with Brahms's liberality with the scissors, than with an extreme, classical, controlling sensibility, as has been presumed in the past. It provides a unique glimpse into the world that Brahms laboured his whole life to keep from the public of his day and the future, the sheer *effort* of his compositional process. To see it is akin to lifting the skin from a flawless, marble classical sculpture to reveal a whirring hive of complex irrational activities, cogs, wheels, regulators, transistors, processors, rubber bands and string just below the untrammelled surface; or, perhaps, to Toto pulling back the curtain to revealing the 'Great and powerful Oz' to be a stuttering old man fiddling with wheels and dials. Such an illicit view of the composer's most private thoughts, his actual process of composing, would have infuriated Brahms. It provides a view of the composer that is about as far removed as possible from the bearded sage lost in thought at the piano; and Brahms would have hated it.

If one looks carefully at the Beckerath painting, it is clear that the composer's strong hands are crossed. For Beckerath depicts him playing the opening of the passionate G minor *Rhapsody* Op 79, which was composed together with the *Regenlied* sonata during a summer sojourn on the Wörther See.[5] Beckerath later wrote that he had painted 'the artist at a moment, when, completely oblivious of his surroundings, he is absorbed in his art'.

PETER SHEPPARD SKÆRVED

xi

Brahms's century

That people are influenced by the period and environment into which they are born was recognized long before sociologists and behavioural scientists demonstrated it: hence the old adage, 'He was a child of his time.' Of course, in a sense everyone is a 'child of their time', but artists are perhaps particularly sensitive to the currents underlying their *milieux*, and especially good at expressing the spirit of their age, irrespective of whether their contemporaries understand them or not.

Johannes Brahms was in many respects a child of the 19th century: his work gave expression to the spirit of the age and he was, after some initial hesitation, understood, or at least respected, by his contemporaries. Indeed, his identification with the period was so strong that following generations found it difficult to accept that his influence might extend beyond his own times. Over a hundred years after his death their reservations have been dispelled, but the question as to what gave rise to them is still of interest.

The year 1848 was a year of revolution in most of the major German states. Unlike Richard Wagner, Brahms took no active part in this revolutionary phase of the 19th century. This was hardly surprising, for he was only

In March 1848, unrest in France spilled over into the German states, where demonstrators demanded freedom of assembly and speech. Republican radicals and the liberal bourgeoisie shared a common aim: national unity. Hastily offered reforms were too little too late: 13 March saw unrest in Vienna, and on 18 March fighting erupted in Berlin. The Bavarian king was forced to abdicate on 20 March. However, the revolution ultimately failed because of divisions among the revolutionaries, and the *bourgeoisie* turned its attention towards industrial expansion.

15 years old at the time, and he lived in Hamburg where the events caused little disturbance. Wagner on the other hand was 20 years older than Brahms, and the restless Saxon had a very different temperament and approach to life from the reserved North German.

The most important and influential years for Brahms were the early years of the second half of the century. In this period following the failed uprisings, the German *bourgeoisie* withdrew from politics to pursue personal ambition; this shift of focus ultimately led to the so-called *Gründerzeit*.

For Germans the word *Gründerzeit* has connotations of greed, flamboyance and vulgar ostentation. The reasons behind the emergence of the *Zeitgeist* of the same name, however, are still a matter of debate, but there was certainly more to the phenomenon than these negative aspects. It was also the manifestation of a tremendous will to succeed. And this great will is very close to the ambition that also drove Brahms and other artists of his time.

The *Gründerzeit* was the epoch of feverish economic activity following the victory over France in 1871 in the Franco-Prussian War. During this period, hundreds of new companies were founded, many of them merely speculative. It ended with a stock-market crash in May 1873. The word is also used more generally for the German version of over-elaborate, mid-to-late Victorian style.

In Brahms's case, however, ambition was often held in check by self-doubt and by an overwhelming respect for the music of his forbears. The pressure on him to undertake large-scale works came not from within, but without, from other people. It was not until relatively late on in his career that he finally made his own decision to tackle these larger forms.

Audiences initially found his First Symphony strange and off-putting, and it was very quickly, and erroneously, categorized as 'classical'. The conductor Hans von Bülow (1830-94) pronounced it the 'Tenth', that is, the first important symphony after Beethoven's nine symphonies. Brahms was duly installed as the 'Successor', and while in some ways he was, in others, as we shall see, he most definitely wasn't.

In the early 20th century the question most frequently asked about Brahms was whether, for all the excellence of his compositional technique, he had not just continued in the tradition of his predecessors, instead of creating something new. Despite the unmistakable individuality of his music, its innovations are not immediately discernible; they are concealed in the highly developed nature of his material. Some of the composers who followed Brahms, most notably Arnold Schoenberg, used his work to find their own musical bearings.

Brahms's innovations were more than partially responsible for the path to 'serialism', and for making the 20th century into the 'age of thematic processes'[6]. Thus it was not simply neat formulation when Albrecht Dümling stated that, 'While it was the fate of Wagner's music to end up as background music to the most horrifying

Arnold Schoenberg (1874–1951) was the defining composer of the 20th century *avant-garde*. Austrian-born, he was a student of Alexander Zemlinsky, whose sister he married. He pushed the chromatic implications of late-19th-century tonal harmony to breaking point with works such as his Second String Quartet, before formulating his own '12-note' system in 1924. He became the focus of an elite circle of the Viennese intelligentsia, and with his two most distinguished pupils, Anton von Webern (1883–1945) and Alban Berg (1885-1935), came to dominate the music of the 20th century. Also an innovative painter, he participated in the first *'Blaue Reiter'* exhibition; in recent years, his graphic work has started to gain similar recognition as his music. He was forced to leave Germany with the rise of the Nazi party, and died in Los Angeles. When told that Serge Koussevitzky did not play his music because he did not understand it, he blurted out: 'Aber, er spielt doch Brahms!' ('but he plays Brahms!')

Richard Wagner (1813–83) redefined the relationship of music to the stage, and to a degree, could be said to be largely responsible for today's conception of multi-media art. As he put it, he was trying to create 'deeds of music made visible'. His concept of total art, of an intimately interwoven fabric of music and theatre, sight and sound, led to the founding of the first theatre built specifically to house the works of only one artist, the *Festspielhaus* in Bayreuth, and his masterpiece, the cycle of operas that make up the *Ring*. This fresh-minted national myth was precisely what the unifying Germany needed. However, in the 20 century this was appropriated by Nazi propagandists, from whose imprint Wagner's oeuvre has never managed to totally escape.

nationalism, it is an irony of history that Brahms and Schoenberg, for all their political conservatism, had a progressive function in the development of music.'[7]

The 'will to succeed' that drove the 19th century could be anything from the straightforward pursuit of profit to an overweening belief in progress. This was deeply embedded in the outlook of the new middle classes, who, after 1848, compensated themselves for their lack of political power with the pursuit of culture. Nowadays we might be tempted to dismiss this pursuit as the pastime of the 'chattering classes', but in the 19th century it was seen as a route to personal liberation, one that transcended the impregnable barriers of class and wealth.

Brahms's own behaviour is a touching example of this: *I invest all my money in books,* he said, *books are my greatest delight; from earliest childhood I read as much as I could and, without any guidance at all, went from the worst to the best. As a child I devoured countless novels about the knights of old, until one day I happened on Die Räuber* (The Robbers), *not knowing it was the work of a great writer . . . I demanded more by this Schiller and so onwards and upwards.*[8] So wrote the 20-year-old Brahms, revealing – in his pride at being an *Autodidakt* and with his focus on upward mobility – just how much he was a 'child of his time'.

Wilfrid Mellers has shown how the gradual disappearance of feudalism is revealed through music, beginning with Jean Philippe Rameau (1683–1764), whose compositions had to appeal to a broad Parisian public. He describes the development of the orchestra as mirroring that of the democratic ideal, and the string quartet even more so, for with it 'music moved out . . . from church and court to the chamber or living room'[9]. Mellers cites Joseph Haydn (1732–1809) as a latent, subconscious revolutionary, and regards Wolfgang Amadeus Mozart (1756–91) as already well involved in the conflict between individual and society. 'He [Mozart] sees the piano concerto as a duality in unity: [and] was subconsciously fascinated by it because it offered an allegorical expression of the separation of the individual (the soloist) from society (the orchestra). But this separation is made in order that the soloist and orchestra can, in the course of the music, evolve a new relationship. The Mozartian concerto only threatens in order to vindicate civilisation. So Mozart remains a classical artist . . .'[10] In the case of Ludwig van Beethoven (1770–1827), the revolutionary intent is explicit. 'There *is* a connection between Beethoven's music and the French Revolution . . . if Haydn and Mozart were incipiently revolutionary composers, Beethoven was overtly so . . . "*My* nobility," said Beethoven, "is *here* and *here*;" and he pointed to his head and his heart.'[11]

Along with Johann Wolfgang von Goethe (1749–1832), Friedrich Schiller (1759–1805) was the most famous and influential German dramatist, poet and historian. He was also the main representative of the *Sturm und Drang* movement; his early works concern the desire for political and individual freedom and other ideals of the Enlightenment.

For Brahms, this political conflict was a thing of the past. He did come into contact with three princely courts: superficially with that of Hanover, where, 'according to Bülow, after a while one was as "bored as a pug on a leash"',[12] with the court at

Detmold, where he had little reason to get annoyed at aristocratic arrogance, though he occasionally managed to do so; and finally with the Meiningen court, where he was treated as an honoured guest. However by the mid-19th century, the well-established middle classes had made princes of their artists. It was considered an honour to be part of the following of one of these great men and to bask in their reflected glory; and being a follower also meant taking sides: Liszt v Schumann, and Wagnerians v (however strange it may sound today) the 'Brahmins'.

The state of permanent conflict and restless striving in which Brahms found himself came on the one hand from the demands he made on himself in conflict with his self-doubt (Nietzsche later, in a deliberate misunderstanding, called this the 'melancholy of

Joseph Joachim (1831–1907) was perhaps the greatest master of the violin of any generation. He came to international acclaim, aged 12, with a performance of the then neglected Beethoven violin concerto in London, conducted by Mendelssohn. His impact on serious music-making cannot be underestimated, ranging from his resuscitation of the violin works of Bach, to his work with living composers, including Liszt, Wagner, Brahms, Schumann, Dvořák, and Clara Schumann. His quartet-playing set a standard of performance and musical ethics never superseded. Initially also acclaimed as a composer, he had a huge impact on Brahms's compositional style, particularly in the early orchestral works, on which he assisted considerably. Joachim's example of total artistic commitment is one to which performers of all instruments still look today.

inadequacy'), and on the other from the inevitable conflict between his desire for a settled, middle-class existence and his instinctual flight from domestic ties. 'F A E' (*frei aber einsam*, free but alone), the motto of his greatest collaborator, the Hungarian violinist and composer Joseph Joachim, and Brahms's inversion, 'E A F' (*einsam aber frei*, alone but free), are both expressions of this conflict within the individual.

Like most members of the middle classes after the failure of the German revolution, Brahms kept almost completely out of politics. He saw no connection between his art and politics, although of course he did, without always intending it, play a role in them.

Brahms gave his first concert on 21 September 1848, the 'year of revolution', when he was 15 years old. There was a cholera epidemic in Hamburg at the time, while on the concert day itself there were street battles in Frankfurt. This may well have reminded Brahms of what he had been told as a child about

Hamburg, Brahms's birthplace

the Napoleonic occupation of Hamburg, although he was not caught up in any unrest himself. On the other hand, at the founding of the German Empire in 1871, Brahms gave way to prevalent popular political sentiment; this is evident in the overblown patriotism of his Op 55, the *Triumphlied* (*Song of Triumph*). However, despite being inspired by the events of 1871, like almost all heroic works of art from this period, it does not draw its material from contemporary events. It was still much more common for musicians and artists to choose scenes from classical antiquity, such as those seen in the paintings of Anselm

Feuerbach (1829–80), or, as in the case of the *Triumphlied*, events from the Bible.

The *Triumphlied* does appear to demonstrate that it is possible for one man to experience deep personal conflicts, to be torn between the demands of form and powerful emotions, while also harbouring a somewhat simplistic political outlook. After composing the piece, Brahms wrote to 'his' Kaiser:

Your Most Serene, Most Powerful and Most Gracious Emperor and Lord,

The achievements of recent years have been so great and so magnificent, that a man who did not have the good fortune to fight in the mighty struggles for Germany's greatness feels all the more impelled to say and to show how blissfully happy he feels to have lived through these great times.

I have tried to give expression to these feelings of joy and gratitude welling up inside me by composing a Song of Triumph.

I have set to music words from the Revelation of St John the Divine, and even if the event it celebrates is obvious, I cannot repress my desire to indicate the particular occasion and intention of this piece through some external sign, if possible by prefacing it with Your Majesty's name.

I therefore venture to express the most respectful wish to be permitted, in token of my veneration, to dedicate the Song of Triumph to Your Majesty when it appears in print.

Your Imperial and Royal Majesty's most humble servant,
Johannes Brahms[13]

Brahms's patriotic sentiment was also revealed some years later in 1888, the year of the accession of the young Emperor Wilhelm II, in a serious argument with his friend, the Swiss writer Josef Viktor Widmann, during which he even went so far as to defend Bayreuth: *But then people criticize everything that comes from Germany. The Germans themselves lead the way. It's the same in politics as in art.*

If the Bayreuth Theatre were in France, it wouldn't need such great works as Wagner's operas to persuade you . . . and the rest of the world to make a pilgrimage there and to wax enthusiastic for something so ideal in concept and execution. Had a Gambetta or a Garibaldi spoken about Alsace in the way our young Kaiser has, the reports in the news-papers would generally have run more or less as follows:

'These are not words, these are living flames that cannot be extinguished! These are weapons no man can resist! Hand back Alsace, it is not only justice, but also this enthusiasm itself that demands and compels it.'[14]

The Swiss writer Gottfried Keller tried to rationalize this contradiction between Brahms's tortured personality and simple nationalism, describing him as 'the son of a free city who, following the immense changes in the political situation, "after 18 short years is the most rabid adherent of the emperor and the House of Hohenzollern there ever was, even in the good old days."'[15] But what is the connection between being 'the son of a free city' and the sudden outbreak of patriotic zeal in an apolitical man?

Claude Rostand, a French biographer of Brahms, dealt with this question in a chapter entitled 'Le milieu historique'. '[Hamburg] remained a city which, protected by its constitution, always stood a little apart from the political ferment in Germany during the 19th century. Hardly any of the unrest caused by the 'struggle for unity', which occupied Germans for 50 years, was felt in Hamburg. In 1848, the year of the great European

In the Treaty of Frankfurt (10 May 1871), France ceded Alsace and parts of Lorraine to the German Reich. The territory, known as Elsass-Lothringen, became self-governing under the Kaiser, who appointed a governor. From the start the population was against incorporation into the Reich: 180,000 opted for France, 50,000 moved there. France became the irreconcilable enemy of the German Reich, an animosity that culminated in the First World War. After Germany's defeat in 1918, the territory was returned to France.

upheaval, the city suffered little more than a mild bout of fever brought on by the presence of Hungarian refugees *en route* for America. Only music appears to have suffered. Impresarios complained about empty concert halls, while shipbrokers were delighted. There was such a rush to book passages that they were sold on the black market. Total political apathy reigned in Hamburg.'[16]

'The Young Eagle' – Johannes Brahms at the age of 20. Drawing by J J B Laurens, 1853

This was the atmosphere in which Brahms grew up. But the century of Johannes Brahms was not only the century of the middle classes, it was, as far as the history of art, music and literature was concerned, the century of the last years of German Classicism, the century of Romanticism and Realism.

It is amazing how quickly Brahms felt at home in this environment. His formal education was somewhat deficient; until he first left Hamburg, in 1853, he knew little of the music of the Romantics, above all of Schumann – *It was only after I had left Hamburg, and especially during my stay in Mehlem* [the summer of 1853], *that I came to know and admire Schumann's music.*[17] Hans Gál describes the youthful Brahms as follows: 'Young Johannes was blond and a Romantic. His idols were Novalis, Brentano, E T A Hoffmann, Jean Paul, and the early works he showed to Schumann were pure, unadulterated Romanticism.'[18]

These, works, indeed, literature in general, were a key influence throughout Brahms's life. Alongside a number of books on music, his large library contained the works of Goethe, Lessing, Lichtenberg, Cervantes, Boccaccio, Shakespeare, Tieck, Byron and Keller, Bismarck's letters and speeches, many anthologies of poetry, and collections of folk music, including some Swedish songs and Broadwood's *English Country Songs*.

The 'salon' was another important feature of Brahms's century; indeed, it could be described as having dominated it. Salons were regular gatherings of friends at private houses

In 1843, the Rev John Broadwood, brother of the piano maker Henry Fowler Broadwood, published one of the earliest collections of English Folksong. In 1880, his niece Lucy Broadwood published a revised and augmented version of this collection, before producing her *English County Songs* in 1893. It was largely thanks to her efforts that the pioneering English *'Folksong Society'* was formed.

to which artists, the 'aristocracy of the middle classes', were invited in order to impress and adorn the gatherings by their presence. Pictures of Brahms's last apartment, which he occupied for many years, reveal a restrained variant of the salon, with its comfortable, yet typical furnishings. Its inventory included a bronze-coloured statue of Beethoven, a white ceramic bust of Haydn, a plaster gypsy couple, six porcelain musicians and nine assorted Romans. There was also a bronze plaque of Bismarck's head, a portrait of Bach and engravings of pictures by Ingres (Cherubini), Raphael (the *Sixtine Madonna*), Leonardo da Vinci (the *Mona Lisa*) and a landscape by Arnold Böcklin. The only articles of intrinsic value in the apartment were the books and thousands of scores, including the autograph manuscript of Mozart's G minor Symphony. Brahms's collection of music manuscripts was second to none, reflecting the broad sweep of his musical interests and expertise.

After Brahms died there was long argument about his estate and the validity of the provisions in his will. Especially noteworthy is that he actually had something to bequeath. Brahms was one of the first composers who managed to accumulate a small fortune from the royalties from his published music. Musicians were now no longer dependent on the *largesse* of upper class patrons and their private commissions. Brahms's music was published and available to any who could afford it; the clientele for his music was the increasing number of musically educated middle-class families. Fifty years of prosperity for the *bourgeoisie* had created a new public for artists. An ever-increasing range of affordable instruments was available to both professionals and amateurs. If 'music [had] moved from the church and court into the home' with the string quartet, then even greater opportunities for domestic music-making had emerged with the invasion of the piano. In addition, the growing popularity of amateur choral groups provided a further resource for composers.

With the slow death of the 'age of patronage' that followed the French Revolution, music publishing moved from being driven by subscription or dedications to ennobled benefactors to being a highly commercial endeavour. It provided music for an increasingly demanding *bourgeoisie*, for whom the ever more popular and affordable piano was a centre of home life. Composers came under pressure from publishers to write music that was easy to play and appealed to the broadest range of abilities, while still humouring the artistic vanity of the performers.

As musical production moved away from the single commission and the patronage and began to cater for a larger, popular market, it also began to be influenced by that market. Brahms was only half joking in the answer he is said to have given a lady who asked, '"How can you possibly manage to write such divine adagios?" – *Well, you know, my publishers order them like that;*'[19] he was often begged to compose easy piano pieces for two or four hands. Yet while this new audience could to some extent dictate Brahms's output, the more positive outcome was that they provided immense new demand for his piano music and songs.

The great need for idols that characterized the German middle classes of the time was now transferred from royalty to artists. Only too aware of his liking for comfort ('cosy' was one of his favourite words), Brahms at times tried to escape from the fêting that came with this admiration. The egocentric artist within him needed to preserve his restlessness. On the other hand, he still toyed with the idea of taking a permanent position, even when his financial situation no longer required it. However, whenever the opportunity presented itself, sooner or later he found an excuse to avoid it. This was also true of marriage. There too, he resorted to excuses. *I missed out on it,* he said to Widmann. *At the point when I would have liked to get married, I couldn't offer a woman what I wanted to offer her . . . At the time when I most felt like marrying, my music was being booed in the concert hall, or at least given an icy reception. I could take it, because I knew exactly how good my stuff was and how quickly things would change . . . But if I had had to go home to my wife, to her anxious, questioning looks, and had to say, 'Another flop' – I couldn't have taken that.*[20]

Were these simply excuses to cover up his inhibition, his commitment phobia? Perhaps, but there was also always an element of self-sufficiency in his behaviour, and this at times restricted him.

Towards the end of his life, Brahms felt that having accomplished all that he had set out to achieve, he had not more to say. Yet, at the very end, with the composition of his *Four Serious Songs* Op 121, the revelation of the works for clarinet, he went beyond anything that had been heard before. The artist within asserted himself one last time. Brahms died a celebrity, a 'maestro' and a musical 'pope'; this man who had lived as a plain, ordinary citizen was buried with all the pomp and ceremony so beloved of the *Gründerzeit*.

'Brahms would have laughed if he could have seen the strutting *hidalgos* in their plumed hats, cloaks and swords who carried him down the worn steps to the street where the glass coach, pulled by its team of six plumed black stallions, awaited him. The wreaths from Hamburg and Vienna covered the coffin.'[21]

He was a 'child of his time', and his time raised monuments to him, but Brahms's music had already transformed the plain, ordinary citizen into a citizen of the world.

Family background and childhood

The Brahms family was spread throughout North Germany. His great-grandfather was a carpenter and wheelwright from Brunsbüttel. His son moved to Meldorf, then Wöhrden and finally to Heide. There he ran a general store, which was eventually taken over by his eldest son, Peter Heinrich Brahms, the composer's uncle. Long after he had become a friend of the composer, Klaus Groth, the North-German dialect poet, recalled, 'My first musical connection with the Brahms family was my attempt to buy a piccolo from a cousin of his. I succeeded, but it was very difficult, as the price was very high and the seller very determined. He eventually succumbed to my powers of persuasion, which I exerted on him over several evenings while we were out playing. The desired instrument, the first musical instrument I ever possessed, cost me every penny I had, four Holstein shillings, I think it was. I must have been eight or nine, Peter Brahms a little younger.'

'His father rented an apartment – in Heide, the main town of Dithmarschen, which at that time had a population of 5000 – not far from my parents' house. He had a shop, though what it sold I could not say, perhaps earthenware and china, kitchen utensils and household goods . . . when he got old he started dealing in antiques, and was passionate, often ruthless, in seeking to make a profit from them, just like a character from a novel . . .'[22]

The younger son, Johann Jakob, Brahms's father, was born in Heide on 1 June 1806. He broke with family tradition by becoming a musician. That his father became a practising instrumentalist, the music world's equivalent to an artisan or craftsman, was a formative factor in the development of the future composer.

Johann Jakob completed his apprenticeship in 1825: 'I Theodor Müller, musician appointed to an official post in Weslingburen in North Dithmarschen, hereby certify that Johann Brahmst of Heide has been apprenticed for three years to the town musician of Heide and for two years to me, in order to learn instrumental music. During his apprenticeship the abovementioned Johann Brahmst has shown himself to be loyal, eager to learn, industrious and obedient, and I therefore hereby declare his apprenticeship completed and release him from all obligations required thereunder. I do not doubt that fellow musicians and all others to whom this document is shown will not only believe the truth of this testimonial and accept the good faith in which it is written, but will also accord the said Johann Brahmst all assistance and goodwill in this regard, both within and beyond his professional duties, such as I consider due in like cases. In attestation whereof I, with the required witnesses, hereby sign and deliver this document. Given this 16th day of December 1825 in Weslingburen. Theodor Müller, Master Musician.'[23]

At the age of 19 Brahms's father went to Hamburg, where he played the flugelhorn in the dance halls of Hamburg Hill, later called St Pauli, Hamburg's equivalent to London's Soho. He was fortunate enough to get a post as bugler in the town guard and worked hard to learn the double bass, which he eventually played in a band that performed at the band stand on the banks of the River Alster. Playing music was a craft, and Brahms's father, with his strong North-German accent, talked like a true craftsman. Famous sayings of his allegedly include: 'Herr Kapellmeister, it's my double bass and I'll play it as loud as I like', and, 'Herr Kapellmeister, a pure note on the double bass is pure chance.' But these 'quotes' are apocryphal, although they have been common currency ever since people first started writing about Brahms.

In 1830, Johann Jacob Brahms was registered as a citizen of

Johann Jakob and Johanna Henrika Christina, Brahms' parents

Hamburg. In the same year he married Johanna Henrika Christina Nissen, who was 17 years his senior. As far as accommodation was concerned, the newly married couple had to make do with the little that they could afford; after a temporary improvement in their circumstances, they ended up in the poor *Gängeviertel*, ('Alley Quarter') of Hamburg. This area was named after the alleyways that used to lead through its city gardens. However, the gardens were by this time little more than a memory, as the area had been densely built up since the 17th century. Here, in a flat consisting of tiny rooms within a house called *Schlüters Hof*, Johannes Brahms was born on 7 May 1833. The house was pulled down a long time ago, but in a photograph from the mid-19th century, it appears to have had an air of tranquillity about it.

Skinny little Johannes probably had to put up with a lot from the toughs of the district. He also suffered from the wretched state of public education in those days, but he at least attended school regularly from the age of six. He played truant just once, and, as an old man he still talked about this event as the *wildest day of my life*.[24]

It was never doubted that Johannes would be a musician, not because he showed talent for music, but because it assumed that a son learnt his father's craft. 'Craft' is a word that surfaces repeatedly in discussing Brahms. His music is sometimes described as 'academic', but perhaps one comes closer to an understanding of Brahms in describing his work as 'highly developed craftsmanship'.

At seven Brahms began his 'apprenticeship', learning the piano with an excellent teacher, Otto Friedrich Willibald Cossell. 'Teach my Johan as much as you know, Herr Cossell,' his father told the teacher in his strong accent, 'then he'll know enough. He'd so love to be a piano player.'[25] Johannes did become a 'piano player', and a superb one to boot.

He learnt quickly and was soon being called upon to contribute to the family finances, playing with his father at night in the taverns and dance halls on Hamburg Hill. Some of his later admirers, especially concerned female admirers, harboured a suspicion that the lax morality of these bordellos and *banlieux* had caused him psychological damage, and that this may have accounted for his inhibitions with regard to women. Perhaps they had a point, for the dance hall world that Brahms encountered could have not have failed to make a deep impression on a sensitive young boy.

Quite apart from these nocturnal performances, Brahms made remarkable progress in his development as a pianist. It was only with great difficulty that Cossell managed to put a stop to a proposed 'child prodigy' tour of America, which would have interrupted his training. He forestalled this by sending his pupil to a new, more famous teacher, the virtuoso pianist and composer Eduard Marxsen. Brahms learnt much from Marxsen, but soon outgrew his teaching too. It was then that the young Brahms began to do what he was still doing as an old man, to 'take musical ideas for a walk'. In 1848 he gave his first solo concert, in 1849 a musical soirée, and by the end of that same year he had completed his first composition, *Improvisations on a well-loved waltz*. It was at this point that it became clear what direction his career was going to take – he was going to be a composer.

After studying in Vienna, Eduard Marxsen (1806–87) made his debut in Hamburg with a concert of his own music. His compositions include the bizarre *Beethoven's Schatte* (Beethoven's Shadow). Marxsen was Brahms's entrée into the Jewish, liberal, intellectual world. He found Brahms's technical precocity astonishing, 'One day I gave him a composition of Weber's . . . at the following lesson he played it to me so blamelessly and so exactly as I wished that I praised him. *"I have also practised it another way,"* he said, and played me the right-hand part with his left hand.'[26]

Later in life, Brahms had very little to say about his early years, indeed he was unwilling to say much about himself at all. Even when writing to a friend such as Hermann Deiters, the philologist, music critic and editor of the *Allgemeine Musikalische Zeitung* who had asked for details of his life, he gives little away.

I really cannot remember any dates and years from my life and I naturally cannot attempt to look them up in old letters etc. Having said that, I hardly need to add that I don't like talking about myself, nor do I like reading things relating to me personally. I think it would be an excellent idea if every artist, great or small, did make a serious attempt to supply personal information – but I never get round to it, it's a pity, but there it is . . .

I do understand, of course, that it's necessary for your work, but with the best will in the world I can't answer your individual questions. Apart from: J B, b 7 March 1834 in Altona (not, as is often stated, 7 May 1833 in Hamburg). I enjoy reading that, and the bit in brackets is correct . . .

Isn't that pretty garden in Bonn called Ermenkeil? Or could it have been Kley? But Ermenkeil or Kley, Detmold or Bückeburg – unless I have got something very fine and serious to tell you, I tend to find my music rather more interesting![27]

Brahms's reluctance to talk about himself has been attributed to his North-German background.

Brahms's birthplace in Schlüters Hof, Speckstrasse 60, Hamburg. The family is said to have lived up one flight, on the left side.

He never got over his irritable taciturnity, even after living in Vienna for years. He was also inordinately shy. He could never overcome his shyness, so he hid it, especially in later life, behind a mask of rudeness, perhaps hoping to make a virtue of necessity. *I am the most unamiable of all the musicians here,* he said with a beaming smile to Florence May in the winter of 1888. 'That I will never believe, Herr Brahms,' she replied, 'never'; Brahms was 'frankly gratified' with this answer.[28]

Brahms's Northern melancholy has been somewhat exaggerated, especially its usefulness as a 'key' to understanding his music, but he was certainly anything but an easy person to get on with. Like all of his generation, he enjoyed social occasions, but he also fled into solitude. He longed for friends, but often offended them, and easily took offence himself:

I don't need to tell you that we can have the best, most excellent opinion of our friends and yet also have good cause to avoid getting on closer, more intimate terms with them. Is it that I'm too boorish, too one-sided, never answer more than a 'Yes' or a 'No' – I think you can answer that one yourself . . .

But do write and tell me about yourself and your affairs. No one will read it with more heartfelt sympathy than your J Brahms.[29]

Brahms's reticence is also of significance for his music, where it is manifested as a reluctance to 'sing his heart out'. But just as Brahms's music also has its 'big tunes', his life too, thanks to the times and the *milieu* in which he lived, was blessed by durable and intense friendships, with both followers of the 'master' and more intimate associates. *I have a very serious and a very simple attitude to friendships and I know what it means and how difficult it is to keep such an intimate relationship as yours with . . . alive and unclouded.*[30] In fact, Brahms never succeeded in keeping his own relationships *unclouded*. But his introduction to the wider world, beyond his childhood sphere, began with friends and quickly led to the decisive friendship and one great love of his life.

In the months before he died, Brahms looked back on his youth, which had been hard, through somewhat rose-tinted spectacles: *And yet I came through it pretty well; to tell the truth, I would not want my life to have been without that period of indigence, for I'm convinced it did me good and was necessary for my development.*[31] This line of thought is also revealed in his description of Ignaz Brüll, a fellow composer now almost forgotten.

He is surely one of the most genuinely talented musicians in the city; he has such a wealth of enviably effortless invention and truly melodious ideas that three of our more prudent composers could have filled their musical piggy banks with them; who knows what he might not have achieved if he had not had such a smooth-flowing life, free of obstacles. A little fight for survival would have done him good, would have shaken him out of his lethargy and released more intensive energy. For that smooth flow characterizes all his works and he takes particular pride in writing in other composers' styles . . . but hardship and adversity would probably have triggered off that indescribable something that can save the charming idyll from monotony and which is essential for the music to carry the hearer away . . .[32]

'His friends used to say that in putting him together Nature had tried out a new recipe and that the experiment had been a failure: too little phlegm had been added to that oversensitive temperament, to that imagination, which could blaze up into a devouring flame, thus destroying the balance that an artist needs in order to live with the world and to create the works for it that . . . it genuinely needs. Be that as it may, Johannes was carried here and there by his inner visions and dreams, as if drifting on the eternal waves of the sea, and it seemed in vain that he sought the harbour where he would at last find the calm and serenity without which the artist cannot create anything. As a result, his friends could not bring him to write down a composition or, if he did write it down, to leave it undestroyed. There were times when, in a fever of excitement, he would compose during the night; full of enthusiasm, he would wake the friend who lived in the next room to play to him everything he had just written down at incredible speed – he would weep tears of joy at the success of his composition – and call himself the most fortunate man on earth, but the next day the splendid music was in the fire.'[33]

The Johannes who is the subject of this text is not, of course, Johannes Brahms, but E T A Hoffmann's eccentric Kapellmeister, Johannes Kreisler, from his *Fantasiestücke in Callots Manier* (*Fantasies after the manner of Callot*). Brahms felt very close to this imaginary character created by this most musical of all Romantic writers. In his youthful enthusiasm, and with bravado that was truly Romantic, Brahms sometimes even signed letters to his friends: *Johannes Kreisler jun.* In those early years he was greatly influenced by Romanticism, and was as a result drawn into his

Ernst Theodor Amadeus Hoffmann (1776–1822) was a polymath, genius and composer. In 1801, his music to Goethe's *Scherz, List und Rache* was premiered in Posen. However, it is as a writer on music that he will be best remembered, most particularly his early, revelatory work on Beethoven, and under the *nom de plume* of 'Johannes Kreisler, Kapellmeister', which were published in the *Allgemeine Musikalische Zeitung* from 1810. His alcoholism probably accelerated the paralysis that killed him.

own personal Romantic purgatorial fire. After the end of this period of his life, which began with his 'going out into the world' and ended with his 'renunciation' of Clara Schumann, he would be a different man. But for the time being he was still 'the Romantic figure wandering dreamily, head in the clouds, through the works of Tieck and his fellow Romantics . . . What he lacks is firmness of character and harmony, but what he has is soul – if one might use the word for the point where the conscious and the unconscious meet. He has a body, in which his tempestuous heart sometimes beats too swiftly, and sometimes too sluggishly, and a face with eyes that look out at us, searching, full of imaginings, full of mystery.'[34]

Throughout his life Brahms retained the typically Romantic dissatisfaction with his own creations; in his will, he wrote, *Likewise I want all manuscript material (unpublished matter) that I leave behind to be burnt. I am doing that myself as far as possible for musical manuscripts; so you will find that there is not much more for you to do.*[35] Brahms first 'went out into the world' with a travelling companion whom he initially admired and looked up to, the Hungarian violinist Ede Reményi. This admiration was probably on account of Reményi's coming from a very different sphere of musical life from his own; his life must have seemed truly exotic to the earnest blond youth from Hamburg. Reményi's statement, 'Today I play Kreutzer Sonata so that sparks fly,'[36] is quoted in almost all biographies of Brahms, with varying degrees of either indignation or malicious pleasure. There can be little doubt that

The Hungarian violinist and patriot Ede Reményi (1828–1906) was born Eduard Hoffmann. After being banished from the Austro-Hungarian Empire for his part in the 1848 Hungarian uprising, he began his solo career in America. He was soloist to Queen Victoria from 1854–9. Like Joseph Joachim, he was a student of Joseph Böhm, but his career was far more international, and included tours to Japan and South Africa. He collapsed and died on stage in San Francisco.

The young Brahms with Reményi

performing this powerful sonata with Reményi had a great impact on the young pianist composer.

Although Reményi and Brahms's own friendship later failed, the Hungarian was responsible for introducing Brahms to Joesph Joachim. Thus began a turbulent friendship which was of decisive importance for the development of both men, and, moreover, for the very concept of what music might be.

The two first met in Hanover in 1853. Brahms and Reményi had made their way to that city by way of concerts in Winsen, Lüneburg, Uelzen and Celle. By this time, Brahms had compositions of his own with him. To earn a living back in Hamburg, he had written easy fantasias under the pseudonym of G W Marks. He also used other pseudonyms and, significantly, high opus numbers; for the pieces he considered good, or at least wanted to acknowledge as his 'own', he usually wrote under the name of Karl Würth.

Although only two years older than Brahms, Joachim was already a celebrated virtuoso. Five years earlier, Brahms had heard him play Beethoven's violin concerto in Hamburg, a piece which Joachim himself, encouraged by Mendelssohn, had rescued from almost complete neglect. Since then Joachim had become leader of the Royal Orchestra in Hanover, which was one of the courts with which Brahms was to become associated: he and Reményi eventually played together before its king, George V.

Initially, however, the two had almost not made it to Hanover at all. They had in fact been on the point of being escorted out of the country by the police, for the Hungarian was thought to be a revolutionary. After Austria's defeat of the Hungarian national uprising, with the help of Russia, in 1849, many Hungarian officers with Austrian death sentences hanging over their heads fled to North Germany, and in particular to Hamburg, from where some left for America. Ede Reményi was among them, and became involved in a concert there organized by the 'Society of Hungarian Refugees': 'Deeply moved by the high degree of warm sympathy and generous support they have received from the friendly citizens of Hamburg, the Hungarian officers presently in this city do not want to depart without expressing their heartfelt gratitude. The grateful memory of the noble people of this great city will live on in Hungarian hearts, even in the wide expanses of America. In order, however, that our presence here shall not pass entirely without trace, our comrade, Ede Reményi, will have the honour of playing a few songs of farewell on the violin in the City Theatre.'[37]

Among the pieces Reményi played at this concert were some 'Hungarian national tunes', a series of melodies that also inspired Brahms. Indeed several years later, on the publication of his *Hungarian Dances* in 1869, Brahms's former travelling companion re-emerged and accused him of plagiarism.

The first meeting between Brahms and Joseph Joachim was what one might call a moment of destiny. Joachim wrote, 'Brahms has a quite exceptional talent for composition and a character that can only develop in its purest form completely shut off from the world. Pure as a diamond, soft as snow . . . His playing is entirely possessed by that intensive fire, by what I would call that fateful energy and precision of rhythm, which tell of an artist in the making. Even now his compositions already contain more of significance than I have seen in any artist of his age.'[38]

Immediately after this first meeting, Brahms and Reményi met up with Joachim in Göttingen. Joachim then wrote ahead to Weimar to announce their imminent arrival there. The town of Weimar, so closely associated with Goethe, was now where Franz Liszt held court. Liszt and his mistress Princess Carolyne zu Sayn-Wittgenstein lived in the Villa Altenburg, surrounded by a whole flock of talented young musicians. Inspired by his antipathy to Liszt, Max Kalbeck, Brahms's biographer and well-known overzealous apologist of all things Brahmsian, gives an amusing and probably not inaccurate description of the internal arrangements: 'The decor of the two storeys and countless rooms of the Villa Altenburg managed to combine church and boudoir, palace and library, hotel and home, studio and an exhibition of curios, the

Franz Liszt (1811–86) styled himself into the defining Romantic artist. Born on the Esterhazy estates near Pressburg, he was an internationally touring virtuoso before his teens; the Erard piano's repeating action was developed to keep pace with his prodigious technique. Liszt created a 'court' around himself in Weimar, and this added to the allure of his charisma and showmanship, which he had culled from his greatest influence, Niccolò Paganini. In addition, he took minor holy orders, becoming the 'Abbé Liszt.' Joseph Joachim led Liszt's orchestra in Weimar for a while, and arranged a meeting with Brahms. This meeting was not a success. Brahms was too shy to play, despite Liszt's having given a brilliant performance of Brahms's Scherzo Op 4, *prima vista*; he was observed asleep behind a pot plant while the older man played one of his own works. Liszt's daughter, Cosima, was initially married to the conductor Hans von Bülow, but left him to marry Richard Wagner.

whole forming a magnificent 'Liszt museum', of which the most remarkable exhibit was the owner himself. With its collection of every tribute that he had ever received, it was a mirror in which the master of the house could preen himself every day. Everywhere he went, he saw himself, he could look at himself from all sides, and each step he took roused the piled-up objects to mute applause . . .'[39]

Liszt gave Brahms a warm welcome, and, in the years that followed – despite the dispute over the 'New German School' of music that was later to estrange them – they always continued to respect each other. *Anyone who has not heard Liszt should keep his mouth shut.*[40] When Brahms refused to play at this first meeting, probably out of shyness, Liszt even played a few of the compositions the young man had brought along with him at sight himself. At this point Liszt may well have been keen to have Brahms as part of his circle, but Brahms was not happy with the idea – *I quickly realized that I didn't fit in. I would have had to lie and I couldn't do that.*[41] Contributing to his feeling of discomfort was the sadness caused by his realization that his travels with Reményi were now over:

If my name wasn't Kreisler, he wrote to Joachim from Weimar, *I would have good reason to despair a little, to curse my love of art and my enthusiasm, and to withdraw as a hermit (clerk?) into the wilderness (of an office), there to lose myself in contemplation (of the files to be copied out).*

Yes, dearest friend, such good reason that my attempt at humour has deserted me already, and I must tell you the bitter truth just as I experienced it.

Reményi is leaving Weimar without me. It is his own decision, my behaviour towards him cannot have given him the least cause, although I have had to put up with his moodiness every day . . . I can't go back to Hamburg, which is where I would now most prefer to take this heart tuned in C-G sharp, without something to show for it; I must have at least two or three of my pieces published so that I can look my parents cheerfully in the eye.

Herr Dr Liszt promised to mention me in a letter to {the publisher} Härtel, so I do have some hopes in that direction. But I would like to ask you, dearest Herr Joachim, to make good the hope you held out to me in Göttingen and introduce me to the artist's life . . .[42]

His great disappointment over his sojourn in Weimar is clear from this letter, but what comes across above all is an impatient desire to prove himself, to find his way to an *artist's life.* Joachim did indeed set him on his way into the world of artists, but he also set him on the way into the one great crisis of both his life and art: he advised Brahms to go on a trip to

Brahms and Joachim, the greatest performer-composer relationship of the 19th century

the Rhineland before going to meet the publishers in Leipzig, and he gave him an introduction to Robert Schumann.

The course of Brahms's friendship with Joachim was to go through several clearly defined stages. At first it was Joachim who 'initiated' Brahms. He was the more experienced, not only as a soloist, but also as a composer. They then started to compete with each other, sending each other exercises to look over and correct, and it was Brahms of course who urged this particular idea on his friend:

Then I would particularly like to remind you of what we have so often discussed and beg you to let us actually get down to doing it. That is to send each other studies in counterpoint. Each of us will send one roughly every two weeks and the other return it, with any comments he can think of, along with his own piece (a week after receiving it, that would be), and so on and on until we know everything there is to know about it.

We are two intelligent, serious-minded people, is there any reason why we should not teach ourselves better, and more enjoyably, than any Professor could. Don't answer this, just send me your first pieces in two weeks' time . . .[43]

Brahms even decreed that there should be an 'overdue box' into which the one who failed to deliver on time would pay a fine from which the other could buy books. As with everything connected with his work, Brahms took these joint studies very seriously: *I just cannot see how the 'circular canon' in your last letter comes by that name. It ends quite reasonably in A major and so can naturally also be played in B major. Only the final phrase permits an entry and that is too short.*

I have written out the same theme for you as a circular canon; I think it's only one when it's like that, don't you?[44]

His letters to Joachim also express a longing for recognition, which would be a constant motif throughout his life – *Your letter, dear Joseph, sent me quite beside myself with joy. I had to run outside because I didn't want to jump for joy in my room . . .*[45]

Brahms had a high opinion of Joachim's compositions, even when it became clear that his work as a composer would never match his outstanding achievement as a violinist. They went on giving duo recitals together until the 1880s. Meanwhile Joachim, not only commented on and corrected Brahms's exercises in counterpoint, but also advised on many of his works as they were developing. This help was not restricted to practical advice about string writing, but ranged across the whole compositional gamut. Indeed for the earlier works his input was fundamental to the end product.

The mutual hyper-sensitivity of the two musicians occasionally resulted in jealousies and rivalry, but this was always dispelled by the profound understanding between them about the nature of music, creativity and interpretation. This didn't mean, however, that there were no arguments. Even as late as 1879, when arranging a concert tour, that they argued about whose name should appear first on the posters. Joachim was the more quick-witted; writing in an earlier argument on precedence, 'Brahms–Joachim, of course, although it will be read as: Joachim–Brahms'.[46]

After decades together, however, a rift occurred between the two friends that proved much harder to bridge. The roots lay in Joachim's character, but equally also in Brahms's earnestness of outlook, which placed justice above all other things, even friendship. Joachim's marriage had broken down, largely because of his abnormal sensitivity and jealousy, and Brahms took up the cudgels for Amalie Joachim (Weiss) Before it came to divorce proceedings, he wrote to Joachim:

Dear friend,

I had some hope, but not much, that your letter would sound more

Amalie Weiss (née Schneeweiss, 1839–99), rose to fame with a performance of Gluck's *Orfeo* at the Hanover Opera, conducted by her fiancé, Joseph Joachim. She left the stage to devote herself to recital work and teaching, winning particular acclaim for her performances of Brahms and Schumann. Brahms's *Geistliches Wiegenlied* Op 91 no 2 was written for the three friends to sing and play together to celebrate the birth of her son, Johannes; it is scored for mezzo-soprano, viola and piano. In 1883, it was Brahms's vocal support of Amalie in the break-up of her marriage that caused a deep rift between Brahms and Joachim. Amalie later toured extensively in the USA.

comforting and hopeful than it does. It has made me decidedly sad and frequently lies heavily on my mind. The two of you had so much in common that suggested a long and happy life together. And now – ! It is difficult to imagine a genuinely serious cause; it is very unlikely that one exists. Brahms goes on to discuss Joachim's jealous accusations *. . . only it is surely much easier for two people to part than to come back together again, just as it is easier to take leave of one's senses than to come back to them . . .* [47]

He even wrote a letter to Amalie Joachim, which she, albeit without his knowledge or consent, submitted to the court as evidence against her husband: *. . . the unfortunate trait in Joachim's character that makes him torment himself and others irresponsibly.* [48]

Deeply hurt as Joachim felt by Brahms's betrayal, he eventually welcomed the opportunity to renew their friendship. Their *rapprochement* began in 1883, when Brahms sent him his Third Symphony, addressing him by his old nickname of 'Jussuf'. Later, on one of his trips to Italy, Brahms saw a statue of St Joachim in the church of Sant'Agostino in Cremona and remarked that it was *. . . quite right that Joachim should have a statue in his honour in the historic city of the violin.* [49]

The northern Italian city of Cremona, on the River Po, has been the 'capital of violin making' since Andrea Amati (1505–77), often called the 'Father of the Violin', established his workshop there. Over the next two centuries, Antonio Stradivari and the Guarneri family established a standard of string instrument making there that has never been superseded.

But, returning to the start of their friendship, it was indeed Joseph Joachim who sent Brahms on his walking tour in the Rhineland in 1853, after his unhappy sojourn in Weimar.

Prior to this, the two of them spent two months together in Göttingen. Joachim had followed courses on history and philosophy at the university there, and it is easy to imagine how readily Brahms, who retained the enthusiasm of the *Autodidakt* all his life, took everything in. They also played and performed together during this time.

Brahms set off on his walking tour in the Rhineland happy at having found a friend with whom he was in harmony in thought and feeling. His contentment was heightened by the Rhine itself, and scenery that epitomized the spirit of the Romantic literature he loved. Today it is not easy to appreciate the intense sensibility of a 20-year-old living in the 1850s. The overwrought tone of conversations and letters from this period must always be seen in context. It was a period of transition between the by then somewhat fractured Romantic outlook and a new realism that was only gradually gaining acceptance. Even when the feeling behind it is genuine, much of the language can come across as insincere emotionalism or overblown rhapsodizing. Thus, for a modern audience, it is perhaps wiser to look to Brahms's music rather than his words to get an accurate sense of his emotional state during that walking tour. The piece that might provide the best 'window' into the mind of the young composer that year is the Piano Sonata in F minor Op 5, which Brahms started in the summer of 1853 and completed that autumn under the aegis of Robert and, most particularly, Clara Schumann. In this sonata, with its highly unconventional opening, the worlds of Classicism and Romanticism meet, and Romanticism triumphs.

During his trip to the Rhineland, Brahms met Wilhelm Joseph von Wasielewski, who was later to be Schumann's biographer, in the house of a wealthy music-lover, *Kommerzienrat* (merchant) Deichmann. Such music-loving merchants, doctors and chemists were typical of this period during which the patronage of the arts completed its shift from the aristocracy to the newly empowered middle classes. It was in Deichmann's house that Brahms first heard the works of Robert Schumann, and Brahms, who was devoted to the writing of E T A Hoffmann, was amazed to

Robert Schumann (1810–56) was the son of a Saxon bookseller who had made a fortune from the German translation of Scott's novels. His command of the wide range of genres was the greatest since Beethoven's; he composed a series of concerti, symphonies, chamber music of all types, *Lieder* and choral works of unsurpassed beauty. His musical sensibility was influenced by his complex psychological make-up, which resulted in various attacks from the age of 23 onwards. His love for his wife, Clara, prevented his mental illness from destabilizing him in earlier years. However, in 1854 he was rescued after attempting suicide in the Rhine. He was hospitalized in Endenich, where he remained until his death, refusing to see his wife and seven children in that time.

discover that Schumann's early works, themselves inspired by Jean Paul and Hoffmann, reflected his own feelings and his ideals of form. So Brahms went to see Robert Schumann in Düsseldorf.

This was a step of immense significance, the effects of which can be seen in his music, especially those works composed under the influence of the first meeting. *What can I say to you about Schumann*, Brahms wrote to Joachim, *should I break out into a hymn of praise of his genius and character?*[50] For his part, Schumann wrote to Breitkopf & Härtel, 'A young man has turned up here whose music has moved us most profoundly; I am convinced he will create a great stir in the musical world.'[51]

Schumann also did something that instantly brought the name of Brahms to the notice of all people with an interest in music, above all to the specialists; he did it with an enthusiasm that aroused scepticism, even in an age when extravagant language was the norm. On 28 October 1853, under the title of 'New

Paths' and signed 'R S', the most celebrated article ever written on Brahms appeared in the *Neue Zeitschrift für Musik*:

'Years have passed – almost as many as I previously devoted to editing this journal, namely ten – since I let my voice be heard in this domain, which is so rich in memories. Despite the exertions of my own creative activity, I have often felt prompted to do so again, as new and important talents have appeared and a new force seemed to be about to manifest itself in music. This new talent can be seen in ambitious works by many of the composers of recent years, even if familiarity with their music tends to be restricted to a limited group. Following the paths of these chosen ones with the greatest interest, I thought that they were, that they had to be, the prelude to the sudden appearance of one who would be called upon to express the highest spirit of this age, one whose mastery would not emerge gradually, but would spring, like Minerva, fully armed from the head of Jove. And he has now arrived – a youth whose cradle was watched over by the Graces and heroes – and his name is *Johannes Brahms*. Only a short while ago he came to me, on the recommendation of a well-known and revered master, from Hamburg, where he had worked in quiet obscurity, although educated by an excellent and enthusiastic teacher in all the most difficult branches of the art. He bore, even in his outward appearance, all the signs that proclaimed, 'here is one of the elect'. Seated at the piano, he began to reveal wondrous realms to us. We were drawn ever more deeply into enchanted spheres. Added to that was the brilliance of his playing, which transformed the piano into a whole orchestra of lamenting and exulting voices. There were sonatas, or rather veiled symphonies – songs whose poetry one could understand without knowing the words, all imbued with a profound, singing melody; individual piano pieces, partly demonic in nature albeit in the most charming way; then sonatas for violin and piano; and string quartets. Each piece was so distinct from the others that they all seemed to spring from different sources. And then it seemed as if he gathered them all together, like a rushing, foaming river, into a waterfall bearing, over its plunging waves, a peaceful rainbow, with butterflies flitting along the bank, accompanied by the voice of the nightingale.

'When the time comes for him to wave his magic wand over the massed forces of choir and orchestra, with their power behind him we will be guaranteed even more wondrous glimpses of the world of the spirit. May the highest of guardian spirits grant him the strength to achieve this; and that he will achieve it is all the more likely as he is possessed by another spirit, that of modesty. His comrades greet him as he sets out into the world, where wounds may await him, but also laurel wreaths and palms; and we welcome him as a doughty fighter for the cause.

'In every age there is a league of kindred spirits. Draw closer together all you who belong there, and let the truth of art shine ever brighter, spreading joy and blessings everywhere.'[52]

What Schumann is expressing here, in the high-flown rhetoric typical of his age, has, despite appearances to the contrary, nothing to do with prophecy. It was his clear-sighted empathy that enabled him to recognize Brahms's genius as musician and composer from the few compositions the 20-year-old had brought with him. Brahms is indeed a composer whose early, sometimes 'clumsier', works contain all the elements of his later mastery. Of course, he did develop – partly in response to the events of his life – but listening to his early works confirms Schumann's instinct; the young man who came to see him was already the 'whole' Brahms.

Schumann's very public praise took Brahms himself by surprise. His initial reaction was one of concern: *Revered Master,* he wrote to Schumann, *you have made me so immeasurably happy, I cannot even attempt to find words to thank you. God grant the fruits of my labours may soon demonstrate to you how much your love and kindness have raised me up and inspired me. The praise you have so openly heaped upon me will have heightened the public's expectations of my works to such an extent that I do not know how I can even start to match up to it. Above all it means I shall have to adopt the greatest caution in the choice of pieces I publish . . .*[53]

Perhaps Schumann's article did Brahms more harm than good in the music world of their time. Schumann himself was an outsider. He had founded the *Neue Zeitschrift für Musik* and edited it up to 1844, but under the editorship of Franz Brendel it had become the mouthpiece of a new trend, *the* new trend in the music of the 19th century. So Brahms may well have been worried that the 'New Germans', and everyone connected with them, might 'excommunicate' him as a result of the article.

The immediate effect of the article, however, seems to have been that everyone was suddenly talking about this unknown young man; 'New Paths' certainly brought the young Brahms into the public eye much more quickly than would otherwise have been the case. Yet he was not overwhelmed by this sudden fame. In this, as in many other things throughout his life, Brahms remained Brahms. He once (in 1885) remarked in conversation that it was sad that young people were in such a hurry to get pieces published and performed before they had been fully worked through:

Ask in Cranz's music shop about all the offers he made me when I wasn't very well known at all! He would have published anything I gave him, sonatas, songs, trios, quartets. At the time I could have used the money, but I gave him nothing. That was the respect I had for printer's ink! I've still got the piece of paper on which Schumann and Joachim wrote down which of my early pieces I ought to publish. Only a few of them ever appeared. Asked if he still had his early compositions, he replied, *God forbid! The stuff's all been burnt. The boxes with my old manuscripts in them stood around in Hamburg for a long time. When I was there two or three years ago, I went up into the attic*

Brahms, c 1856 'seated at the piano, he began to reveal wondrous realms to us'

— the whole room was beautifully papered with my music, even the ceiling. I only had to lie down on my back to be able to admire my sonatas and quartets. It looked very good. Then I ripped everything off — better me than someone else — and burnt it along with all the rest.[54]

Beneath the avuncular tone Brahms adopted for such conversations was a gravity that was essential to his character as man and artist. He took his talent very seriously. As Thomas Mann put it, 'For talent, ladies and gentlemen, all you down there in the stalls, talent is not an easy thing, not something you can dabble with, it is not simply a skill. At bottom, it is a *need*, a critical awareness of the ideal, a refusal to be satisfied, which, not without torment, creates and refines its skill . . .'[55] Brahms himself said, *It doesn't just come to you like that! . . . Do you think that any of my few decent songs came to me just like that, the finished article? I had to slave away at them!*[56]

In November 1853, with Schumann's encouragement, Brahms went to Leipzig to see about getting his works published: *Mynheer Domine (sic),* he wrote to Schumann, *I'm sure you will forgive the humorous form of address from a man whom you have made immensely happy and glad.*

And now for the best. Thanks to your warm recommendation, my welcome in Leipzig has been much friendlier than I expected, and certainly than I deserve. Härtels said they would be delighted to print my early pieces . . .

Might I dedicate my Opus 2 to your wife?[57]

Brahms's request to be allowed to dedicate his Sonata for Piano in F sharp minor Op 2 to Schumann's wife is his first recorded mention of Clara Schumann. She was there when Brahms first visited Düsseldorf and there is no doubt that she made a profound impression on him. She was a 34-year-old mother of six, but this does not seem to have diminished her otherworldly charm. For an idealistic young man such as Brahms, she must have seemed the epitome of cultivation, exotic beauty and intelligence; not a vision from his imagination, but the living embodiment of his Romantic yearnings and intellectual aspiration.

Brahms was not initially conscious of all this. He was exhilarated at being received in the house of two great artists, and was both perturbed and uplifted by the implicit challenge to his creative powers; it was still very much a case of being faced with rather than belonging with the Schumanns. However, he drew inspiration from the sense of having arrived at the right place, and there was an immediate effect on his productivity.

'Kreisler' (i.e. Brahms) 'is the most amazing person. Hardly has he delighted us with his trio, than he has finished three movements of a sonata for two pianos, which seem to me infinitely superior.'[58] This was written to Joachim by Julius Otto Grimm, one of Schumann's pupils, in 1854, a week after Brahms had journeyed to Düsseldorf to offer his support to a troubled Clara. On 27 February 1854 Robert had thrown himself into the Rhine. The crew of a river boat had pulled him out alive, and he had then been taken to a clinic in Endenich that specialized in nervous disorders. Brahms felt he was living through the traumatic experience with Clara. *Wretched weather and, unfortunately, worse news from Bonn make things bleak for me . . . Our last hope has proved vain . . . Frau Schumann is suffering terribly.*[59] In addition to all of this, Clara Schumann was pregnant. Her seventh child Felix was born on 11 June 1854; some believed that Brahms was the father.

The origin of this rumour lay in the obvious reality that Clara

Robert and Clara Schumann, daguerreotype by Johann Anton Völlner, Hamburg 1850

Clara Schumann (née Wieck), 1819–96, was the daughter of the music teacher and piano manufacturer Friedrich Wieck (1785–1873) who taught Hans von Bülow and Robert Schumann. A child prodigy pianist and composer, she gave her debut at the Leipzig Gewandhaus aged nine, and her first European concert tour in 1831–2. In 1837, Robert Schumann, who had been living in the family house since 1830, asked to marry her, but was virulently opposed by her father, who was probably worried at the prospect of losing the best advertisements for his teaching and pianos in one fell swoop. After this issue was resolved through the courts, the two moved to Dresden, where she managed to balance the demands of a large family with touring, composing and teaching. Her workload redoubled with Robert's illness and death, which forced her to increase her touring schedule to pay for all her children, whom she adored, forcing her to spend much time away from them. She regularly appeared in the United Kingdom, and was concertizing until 1891. Clara actually wrote her last work, *Drei Romanzen* Op 22, in 1853, as her husband had counselled that she could not combine motherhood, composing and performing. In recent years, however, her mature works have been revived and she is now seen as having had a decisive impact on chamber music, particularly on the music of Brahms. A number of his pieces, particularly his Sonata in A major Op 100, which is dedicated to Clara, reveal not only the influence of her poetic pianism, but also her finely spun compositional style.

and Brahms had fallen in love. Maybe even Robert Schumann himself was a little in love with this genius with the baby face and blond hair. On top of this, little Felix – and there is a surviving childhood photograph of him – appeared to have the same expression of defiance, the same pouting lower lip, as Brahms.

In 1926, Clara Schumann's grandson penned a romantic account of the affair, under the pseudonym of Titus Frazeni. According to his story, on the evening of Brahms's first visit, Clara followed him to the inn where he was staying and 'a power blazed up which brooked no resistance'.[60] Unfortunately for the story, however, little Felix came into the world three weeks too soon for the accusation to be correct. The grandson is now thought to have attacked Clara Schumann out of revenge for not having bequeathed any of Robert Schumann's effects to his branch of the family.

Had this night of passion actually occurred, would the young Brahms really have been able to play as freely in Robert Schumann's presence as he actually did? In addition, his letters, which fluctuate between poles of hope and despair, help to discredit this legend; it is a fabrication. However, even if the story is untrue, it is undeniable that the various stages of Brahms's love for Clara Schumann had a profound effect on both his life and work. This is well documented, for although Clara and Brahms later exchanged letters with the declared aim of destroying them, fortunately for later generations, they found it impossible to part with them all.

A few weeks after the birth of Felix, Clara went to a spa to recuperate, but soon resumed her touring activity as a concert pianist, which was vital for the upkeep of her large family. In the meantime, Brahms went to South Germany vainly hoping to find a clinic for Robert. At this point their correspondence began; despite now being much reduced by the loss of so many letters, it clearly delineates the course of their relationship. This can almost be intuited from merely reading the changing forms of address: *Dear Madam*, it starts, then *Dearest Friend, My most beloved Friend, My most dearly beloved friend, My beloved Frau Clara, Dear Clara*.[61]

The first letter after they had been seeing each other every day in Düsseldorf was written in August 1854. It ran:

Dear Madam,

On this trip I have not yet managed to feel as unreservedly happy as one ought to feel on a walking tour, and as I usually do.

I could turn back at any moment and would not be tempted to leave Düsseldorf again for the rest of the summer.

Oh, how can I abandon, even for a short time, our lively and uplifting togetherness, making music with you, and hearing news of your beloved husband?

I'm often at odds with myself; that is, Kreisler and Brahms quarrel with each other. Usually each one has his own definite opinion and manages to put it across. This time, however, they were both quite confused, neither knowing what he wanted; it was quite a comic sight. The tears almost came to my eyes.

I've got a bit farther now, by train, and am in Esslingen already. As I write to you there's a whole Eichendorff performance going on outside: dark midnight, the sleepy murmur of the fountains, a babble of distant voices, and deep melancholy in my heart . . .[62]

Other letters followed that year:

Dear Madam,

I can stand it no longer; I'm coming back, this very day. I arrived here this morning, intending to wait until 9 o'clock in the evening to see if there was a letter from you, then continue on to Tübingen, but I just can't . . . I've decided to go home and play and read by myself until you come and we can do it together . . .[63]

By this stage 'home' already means Düsseldorf with Clara Schumann. *I feel a profound yearning to see you again, dearest; do not keep us waiting longer than necessary . . .*[64]

Since I spent that wonderful summer with you, I find it impossible to stay here (Brahms is writing from Hamburg). *Please forgive that word 'wonderful'. It was a wonderful summer for me, despite the seriousness of what happened, I will never forget it. Perhaps the winter will be infinitely more beautiful; it simply must turn out to be just as good.*

Fare you well, dearest lady, and think kindly of

> *Your*
> *Johannes Brahms.* [65]

Dearest Friend,

You use the intimate 'Du'! How affectionately it looks up at me from the page. A thousand thanks! I cannot look at it or read it enough. If only I could hear it; seldom have I felt the absence of the spoken word so strongly as when I was reading your last letter . . . [66]

I would like to write to your dearest husband about the summer we have spent, I could talk to him for hours on end about it without causing the slightest hurt or distress . . . [67] Brahms, the younger man, continues to use the formal *Sie* to Clara, though at one stage he does find a way of using the familiar *Du* through the adoption of a fairy-tale persona:

The letters I have written have been too horrible, I realize that now. I'll write you another, copied from the Arabian Nights, *it describes the state I'm in perfectly, despite the fact that the writer was a prince and I'm a composer.*

So then, after Johannes has wished you good night, like a good boy, the Brahmin drags himself from his bed, takes up quill *and paper and writes (in answer to your last letter):*

In the Name of God, the Merciful, the Compassionate. Thy letter, oh my mistress, has arrived, pouring balsam on a soul tortured by longing and desire, bringing healing to a sick and broken heart. Thy weary slave (how lovely!) has devoured every gracious word and near thy head, o my shatelain! my state is that described by the poet:

'My heart is troubled and filled with sorrow, sleepless my eyes and

tired my body, short my patience, but lasting the separation, my mind in confusion and my heart lost.' (Oh!) – My lament cannot extinguish the fires of despair, but it does bring relief to a man racked by yearning and suffering caused by his separation from the object of his desires.

Would to God I could tell thee with my own lips, instead of sending this letter, that I am dying of love for thee. More I cannot say for the tears that fill my eyes. Fare thee well.

Camaralzaman Ibn Brah.

When Ibn Brah had finished the letter he had written with sighs and tears, he took it to the Prussian Mail, dropped it in the letter box and said, 'I beseech you, take this letter to my beloved mistress and give her my greetings.'

J B[68]

The Schumann Children

And then:

What have you done to me? Can't you remove the spell you have cast over me?[69]

This was January 1855, and Brahms was back in Düsseldorf, but Clara had left for Rotterdam, where she was to play. Brahms followed her there. Afterwards: *What a lovely letter your last one was! But an 'embrace' from Amsterdam to Düsseldorf has to be a long-distance affair. Truly harmless and very moral.*[70]

From Brahms in Düsseldorf with Clara's children:

My darling Clara,

Your last two letters were waiting for me when I came down this morning. The one with the posy, the stalks look like silk . . . Yesterday and today the boys regaled themselves with

Brunswick cake. I give them your kisses, but I'd also love to return their kisses to you! [71]

Clara, dear Clara,

A letter from you at last, I have been hoping for one long enough . . . In my love for you I am becoming more and more joyful, more and more calm, every time I feel your absence more strongly, but my longing for you is almost a joyful longing, that is the way it is, it is a feeling I had once before, but never so heartfelt. [72]

I begrudge every word I write to you that does not speak of love. [73]

Brahms had never before written such words, nor would he again, after it was all over. *I have become very emotional, but only when I am thinking to myself; it quickly goes when I start writing.* [74]

Brahms had abandoned himself to his passion; Clara, whose letters from this period have not survived, was also greatly moved by the young man's intense devotion. This can be seen very clearly in her later letters when Brahms has been over-strict in his application of a 'renunciation':

'Am I going to get a long letter from you some time soon? It would be like a Christmas present, a delight – things are serious enough for me, as you know. Take your time over it, dear Johannes – an extra minute and a few friendly words will delight the recipient.

Goodbye, dear Johannes. It was lovely to see you, only the visit was so short – almost a fleeting vision.

Warmest greetings.
Your Clara.' [75]

But back in May 1856, Brahms was still pressing his suit with Clara; and from now on his letters to her are in the familiar *Du* form:

'I don't want to take advantage of the recent surprise attack on me straight away.' The one with the 'Du', I mean. I decided I didn't want to exploit your momentary kindness and love, you might be unhappy with it later on. That's why I've been writing to you in the 'Sie' form until

now. This story of siege and conquest must have something to do with the unanswered question? Does it?[76]

What 'unanswered question' was this? Could it have been whether, if Clara were one day free, she would be free to marry Brahms? The final years of her marriage to Robert Schumann were years when she had to subordinate herself to the worry about a sick man suffering from mental illness. How understandable, then, that she should feel attracted to the young Brahms, who worshipped her and at the same time rejuvenated her troubled spirit:

My beloved Clara,

I wish I could write to you as tenderly as I love you, and give you all the love and care I feel you deserve. I am so immensely fond of you, more than I can say. I could just go on and on calling you 'darling' and all sorts of endearments like that, without ever tiring of it. If it goes on like this, eventually I'll have to put you in a glass frame, or save up and have you set in gold.[77]

This letter, which also contains the words *your letters are like kisses to me*, is the last before the long-expected and yet, for both Clara and Brahms, still unimaginable death of Robert Schumann. At the beginning of July 1856, Brahms and Clara spent a few days together, and at the end of the month, Robert Schumann died in the clinic in Endenich. In the days before his death, his wife and friend went to see him; Brahms had visited him alone some weeks earlier:

I was with Schumann on his birthday (8 June), and I found a sudden and remarkable change in him compared to how he was during my previous visit. After that Frau Clara came back from England, and on her arrival was met by even worse news from Endenich. A week before his death (Wednesday) we received a telegram and I was the one to read it. It said something like, 'If you want to see your husband while he is still alive, hurry here without delay, though I have to tell you that his appearance is distressing.'

We drove there . . . I went in to him, and saw him, however, just as he was having convulsions. He was greatly agitated, so both I and the doctors advised Frau Schumann against going to him, and persuaded her to return home. Schumann was just lying there, taking nothing more than wine and jelly from a spoon.

But Frau Clara's suffering during those days was so great that on Saturday I felt I had to suggest that we go to see him again. Now and forever we thank God that she did so, for it was absolutely essential for her peace of mind. She was able to see him on Sunday, Monday and Tuesday morning, and then he died on Tuesday afternoon at four o'clock.

I will surely never again experience anything as moving as the reunion of Robert and Clara. At first he lay there for some time, his eyes closed, and she knelt beside him, more calmly than one would believe possible. But after a while he recognized her, as he did again the next day. Once he plainly wanted to embrace her and flung one arm right round her.

Of course he had been unable to speak for some time, you could just make out (or perhaps imagine you could) disjointed words. But even that must have made her happy. He often refused the wine that was offered him, but from her finger he sometimes sucked it up eagerly, at such length and so passionately that one knew for certain that he recognized the finger.

On Tuesday at noon Joachim arrived from Heidelberg. That delayed us somewhat in Bonn, otherwise we would have arrived before he passed away; as it was, we arrived half an hour afterwards. I felt just as you [Julius Otto Grimm] *did when you read about it; we should have breathed more freely because he was released, and yet we couldn't believe it . . .*[78]

Two sentences in this letter provide important indicators of Brahms's feelings at the time. They also do much to explain his subsequent attitude: *I will surely never again experience anything as moving as the reunion of Robert and Clara,* and, *we should have breathed more freely because he was released, and yet we couldn't believe it.* The second sentence expresses the grief Brahms felt at the death of the friend he so admired. It acquires new meaning, however, when one realizes that after his death Robert Schumann would have a more decisive effect on the lives of Clara and Brahms than when he was alive, if barely conscious of what was going on around him. Brahms had always been a rather serious character and Clara Schumann's reunion with her dying husband must have haunted him for the rest of his life. Any intimacy they might later have enjoyed was forever stymied by the complex feelings of shock and, perhaps, guilt, which Schumann's death engendered.

Brahms's stormy C minor Piano Quartet Op 60 was his most explicit and passionate statement of his ill-starred love for Clara Schumann. As he made clear in letters to his publisher, Simrock, this work was linked to his identification with the plight of the 'hero' of Goethe's seminal *The Sorrows of Young Werther* (1774) and Werther's hopeless passion for Charlotte. Seen in this light, the quartet comes close to being programmatic music, particularly as it appears to finish with a despairing coda and two gunshots, perhaps Werther's suicide. Curiously, Brahms himself at one point appears to have been suggesting that Simrock take advantage of the then cutting-edge technology of three-colour printing to have a picture on the title page of himself wearing Werther's signature yellow waistcoat, with a gun to his head.

The period in Brahms's life that ended with the death of Robert Schumann has often, and justifiably, been called his 'Werther years' (after Goethe's novel of unrequited love, *The Sorrows of Young Werther*). Beside the many parallels with the novel – for example Clara's children, whose welfare Brahms continued to look out for even after Robert's death – we have Brahms's own testimony that he knew his *Werther*: *I have sent you the quartet purely as a curiosity. As an illustration of the man in the blue coat and yellow waistcoat in the last chapter.*[79] This refers to the following passage from the novel: 'He had shot himself while sitting at his desk, then had slumped down and twisted himself out of his chair in his convulsions. He was lying on his back, against the window, fully clothed in his blue coat and yellow waistcoat, with his boots on.'[80] But Brahms no more put a bullet through his brain out of despair over Clara Schumann than Goethe had over Charlotte Kestner.

'As with the young Goethe,' wrote Hans Gál, 'the real mystery about Brahms is the way he is ready to take flight at any moment. It is a motif which is repeated every time he becomes emotionally involved with a woman.'[81] This pattern is not only repeated in all his emotional involvements, it can also be seen, as discussed, in his desire for and rejection of a permanent position, and in his choice of summer residences. He grew very fond of all of these, but didn't spend more than a few summers in any one of them. There was almost a rhythm to this erratic behaviour.

The motive for his inability to commit might lie in his subconscious recognition that his creativity pre-required a dynamic between calm and restlessness. His avoidance of commitment was perhaps a kind of voluntary phobia. The 'post-romantic' Brahms no longer bore Joachim's romantic motto 'FAE' (*frei aber einsam*, free but alone), emblazoned on his standard, but it still remained a leitmotif of his life, despite the lively intercourse with friends, and his espousal of its pendant, 'FAF' (*freie aber freudlich,* free but joyful). Indeed many of these friends were scarcely more than like-minded acquaintances.

Besides the pieces composed in 1853 and 1854, inspired by the euphoria of his new acquaintance with the Schumanns,[82] Brahms did not produce any other new work in this period, until after his separation from Clara. During this time, he was far from idle, but he had had to earn a living, and composing and giving music lessons could not support his immediate needs. Therefore, with Joachim's help, he was engaged for a number of concerts; with the result that for some years to come, his reputation as a concert pianist exceeded his fame as a composer.

Brahms performed in many German cities, including

Joseph Joachim and Clara Schumann; maybe they are performing Clara's exquisite *Drei Romanzen* Op 21. Reproduction of lost drawing by Adolph von Menzel, 1853

Hamburg, where he performed Mozart's D minor Concerto on the eve of the 100th anniversary of the composer's birth. On that occasion he played 'from a hand-written score, probably the one he had had since he was a boy, when he was in the habit of making a piano score from the various parts of major works of music of which he was particularly fond.'[83] In this activity we can see evidence of another defining influence on Brahms, his commitment to the study of works of the past: *Perhaps, after all, I'll have to tell you about my library. I have a Beethoven manuscript! A copy of his last A flat major Sonata* [the 'Hammerklavier' Op 106], *with corrections and titles written in by His Own Hand!*[84] This was far from atypical of the time. Printed music was still very expensive, and many musicians learnt works by copying them out. Brahms's Russian contemporary, César Cui, for example, began his musical education by copying out works by Chopin and Schumann.

Brahms's music was often stimulated by a poetic idea, which provided the initial spark of inspiration for a piece or a movement, without it ever becoming 'programme music'. At the end of 1853 he wrote to his publisher:

Herewith the promised 'Sonata' at last. I have washed it well so that now it's clean and fit to show its face in public . . . Nb I have already sealed the package with the 'Sonata' and do not want to waste any more time; I therefore ask you to have the following little verse set at the top of the first Andante, in parentheses and in small print. It is perhaps necessary or at least convenient for the understanding of the Andante:

('As evening falls, in the pale moonlight,

Two tender, loving hearts unite

In a rapturous embrace.') Sternau

Nb, {this is for} over the first Andante; there are two in the 'Sonata'.[85]

The composer Albert Dietrich, with whom Brahms and Schumann had collaborated on the 'FAE' Sonata for Joachim, wrote an account of Brahms during his first Düsseldorf period; his description tells us much about Brahms's work practices. 'I remember one soirée in the house of the hospitable and music-loving Euler family. Brahms was asked to play; he performed Bach's Toccata in F major and his own Scherzo in E flat minor Op 4 with wonderful power and mastery. As was his habit at the time, he was quivering with excitement and hummed the melody, keeping his head bowed low over the keys and modestly rejecting the enthusiastic praise that followed. Everyone was amazed at him and his outstanding talent; we young musicians especially were full of the profound artistic impression made by his playing – always distinctive, powerful and, where necessary, extremely delicate – and by his wonderful compositions. There was a general desire to hear him again.

'Soon after that there was an excursion to Grafenberg Hill. Brahms was of the party and showed all the charming and artless freshness of youth. Joking and teasing, he pulled up turnips from the field and playfully offered them, carefully cleaned, as refreshment to the ladies dressed up in their finery. On the way back the two of us, as the only musicians in the party, fell into conversation. Amongst other things, he told me that when he

Albert Dietrich (1829–1908) studied, with Moscheles and Schumann. In 1853, he collaborated with Schumann and the young Brahms on a 'greeting' sonata based on Joseph Joachim's motto F-A-E (*frei, aber einsam*). He was the Bonn city music director from 1859, and published a memoir of Brahms in 1899.

was composing he liked to remember folk songs and then the melodies would come unbidden. Thus in the 6/8 finale of his C major Sonata Op 1 he had had the words of 'My heart's in the Highlands' in mind, and in his F sharp minor Sonata Op 2, he based the melody of the second movement on the words of an old German song, *Mir ist leide, dass der Winter Beide, Wald und auch die Heide, hat gemachet kahl* (It is sorrowful to me, that winter hath both wood and heath laid bare).'[86]

After the separation from Clara, following Robert Schumann's death in the summer of 1856, the tone of Brahms's letters to her changed. But in the months immediately following his death, they were still very close. In August and September that year, they took a holiday in Switzerland, with Schumann's two sons, Ludwig and Ferdinand, Brahms's sister Elise and, initially, Joseph Joachim. Their journey started and finished at Schumann's resting place.

A month after the holiday, in a letter of 28 October 1856, Brahms was still full of sympathy: *Your dear letter arrived yesterday, my Clara; my most ardent wish is to be able to comfort you, but how do I do it? What you are suffering seems to me so ineffably hard that the very idea simply disappears . . .*[87] Brahms had not yet given up hope of being able to console Clara; later in the letter he says, *Let it be a cheering thought that every time we see each other again I am more and more wholly yours.* But as he came to understand the inevitability, the necessity of renunciation and freedom, a different tone crept into his writing. Had this letter not come from Brahms, it might sound like mockery. What it actually reveals, is that Brahms was clearly trying to convince *himself* of what he writes to Clara:

Passions are not an inherent part of mankind. They are always exceptions or deformities.

Anyone in whom they exceed normal bounds must consider themselves an invalid, and must take care of their life and health with medicine.

The beautiful, the true human being is calm in joy and calm in pain and sorrow. Passions must quickly fade, or they must be driven away.[88]

Brahms wrote this letter from Detmold.[89] He had visited the tiny principality at Whitsuntide in 1857, and had been so well liked that a longer stay had been arranged for that autumn. Detmold was typical of the many small German states still governed by princes or dukes who had managed to retain their role as patrons of the arts, even after their real political significance had vanished. The composer and librettist Albert Lortzing (1801–51) had lived there from 1826–33, and in 1825, the new theatre had opened there with a performance of Mozart's *La Clemenza di Tito*. Princess Friederike, sister of the reigning prince, had met Brahms at Clara Schumann's house in 1855. He now gave piano lessons to her and to the ladies of the court, and also conducted the *Kleiner Gesangverein* (Chamber Choral Society) in the castle. Working with this little choir would be important for Brahms both as composer and performer:

The pleasures of Their Serene Highnesses leave me no time to think of myself. In fact I am pleased they are making such demands on me, since I am profiting from many things that I lacked until now.

How little practical knowledge I have! Rehearsing the choir has revealed great weaknesses; it will not be without benefit to me. My things are certainly written in an excessively impractical way![90]

He also made a good friend in Detmold, the leader of the orchestra, Carl Bargheer, with whom he resumed his favourite activity of going for walks. In a sense, the Teutoburg Forest was a precursor of the Vienna Woods or the mountains near Lake Thun in Switzerland, where Brahms would later 'take his musical ideas for a walk'.

Adapting to society, however, was something that was never a priority to Brahms, even at the Detmold court. His answer to criticism of his behaviour by friends is said to have been a plain, *Oh, that's all just a load of prissy nonsense.*[91] Carl Bargheer, like his other friends, also found him to be frustratingly unforthcoming about his work. '. . . Brahms never talked about his pieces before they were finished. Just once, when I came across him one midday writing music, with everything in the room – piano, tables, bed, chairs – covered in sheets of manuscript paper, which he, a great early riser, had written that morning, he said to me, *I'm just arranging the Serenade* (Op 11, originally an octet) *for orchestra, it'll sound better like that.* When I replied, "Then it'll be a symphony," Brahms said, *If anyone dares to write symphonies after Beethoven, then they'll have to look quite different.*'[92]

In 1854 Brahms wrote to Joachim: *The eagle soars alone, but the crow tribe clusters together; God grant that my wings may grow vigorously and the time will come when I belong to the former species.*

Recently the 9th Symphony was given at a concert in Cologne and I went with Grimm; it was the first time I'd heard it.

It was not mere chance that his remark about his wings growing vigorously came immediately before the reference to Beethoven's Ninth. At the same time he talked of a sonata for two pianos: *I would really like to put my D minor Sonata on one side for a long time. I have often played the first three movements with Frau Schumann. (Improved.) {But} actually, even two pianos aren't enough for me.*[93]

No, two pianos were not enough, and although at the beginning of the 1870s he was still maintaining, *I will never compose a symphony! You have no idea how people like us feel when we hear a giant like that (Beethoven) breathing down our necks all the time,*[94] the 'never' had actually already gone by the board many years earlier.

Whatever his anxiety about it might be, he could not let go of the idea of writing a symphony, especially since his close encounter with the 'form-shattering' power of the giant Beethoven in that performance of the Ninth in 1854.

In the end, the sonata for which two pianos were not enough did not become his first symphony, but eventually metamorphosed into his first Piano Concerto Op 15. The concerto was the product of a long and extremely laborious process. Up until this point Brahms had had no practical experience of the capabilities and limitations of a large orchestra. In Detmold he had occasionally been able to work with the court orchestra, but it was really modest in scale compared to the demands this work made from the outset.

A certain healthy scepticism is perhaps justified with regard to much that has been read into this extraordinary piece. Nonetheless, it is certainly undeniable that all the psychological strains and stresses Brahms went through in the years between 1855 and 1857 are reflected in this work. The words *Benedictus qui venit in nomine domini (blessed is He that cometh in the name of the Lord)* written over the theme of the *Adagio* in one of the sketches, most likely refer to Robert Schumann.[95] But certainly, the tensions of these years should not be seen as the sole driving force behind the piece. One might be tempted to call the concerto Brahms's *Werther,* a work which he, like many of his and previous generations, had referenced for other pieces; there is certainly a lot to be said for the idea that in writing it he 'got something out of his system'. However, any investigation into the psychological background to the piece should not be allowed to obscure the fact that Brahms as a composer was exceptionally preoccupied with problems of form; he could get caught up in and, if they proved insoluble, enraged by them. Sections of the concerto were passed back and forth between Brahms and Joachim, who had earlier advised on the orchestration of the aforementioned serenade:

Please send my concerto as

J W von Goethe (1749–1832), the greatest German literary figure of his era, studied law in Leipzig, worked as a journalist, an actor and a manager of a theatre, and was a court official to the Duke of Weimar. His works include plays, novels, poetry, songs and essays ranging from natural history to religion. His most acclaimed work, *Faust,* was completed towards the end of his life.

well, if possible; I wouldn't ask if I didn't need to finish it off in every sense of the expression. Another thing I'd like to ask you is whether the passage for solo horn in the first movement could be played by the first horn on both occasions? The third horn is often pretty lousy (eg in Hamburg, Elberfeld) . . . The piccolo is used in at most three bars, should it be left out entirely or would it sound good joining in in the finale? Initially I had the second theme in the Rondo, where it comes for the second time in D minor, an octave higher (in octaves) . . .[96]

However banal these pragmatic questions might appear, they are far from unimportant. Another letter to Joachim reveals more of the hopes and uncertainties of the 24-year-old composer:

Yet another draft! It's probably very unreasonable of me to send it to you. I don't even know how I've found the time to write myself, I can't do much more than send you hurried greetings and once again ask you to look kindly on the movement.

If you're willing and have the time, do write me a few words right away to say whether you think my labours have not been entirely in vain and whether it might turn into something worthwhile. My judgment and control over the piece seem to have vanished.[97]

The piece was finally given its first performance in Hanover on 22 January 1859, with a second, important performance in the Leipzig Gewandhaus on 27 January 1859. It was an unmitigated disaster. *Still utterly intoxicated with the edifying delights that the sight and converse of the sages of our city of music have been bringing to my eyes and ears for several days now, I take up this sharp and hard steel nib of Sahr's to tell you how it came to pass that my concerto was a brilliant and decisive – flop.*[98] This was sheer gallows humour; he was surely convincing no one when he went on in the same letter, *This flop, by the way, has made absolutely no impression on me,* but the mixture of self-criticism and self-confidence with which it then continues is very characteristic of Brahms: *. . . and the bit of a bleak, bad mood following it faded when I heard a C major Symphony by Haydn and the* Ruins of Athens [by Beethoven]. *In spite of all this, the concerto will*

The Leipzig 'Gewandhaus' concerts are named after the Leipzig Cloth Merchants' Guildhall in which they were held in the mid-1700s. In 1781, the concerts relocated into a new hall, and subsequent music directors included Mendelssohn, Gade and Reinecke. In 1879, Joachim gave the premiere of the Brahms Violin Concerto in the old hall (pictured), which was replaced with a larger hall in 1884. This hall was destroyed by aerial bombardment in 1943, and replaced with a modern structure in the 1970s.

be a success some day when I have improved its anatomy, and a second one will certainly sound different.

I believe this is the best thing that can happen to one; it forces one to think about really pulling oneself together and gives one heart. At the moment I'm just experimenting and still groping.

But the hissing was surely a bit much?

Brahms was proved correct in everything he says here. The concerto only had to wait for its Hamburg premiere on 24 March of the same year to find success, and *a second one* did indeed *sound different*, though it was a good 20 years before it finally appeared (in 1881).

Brahms's activity as a composer was by no means restricted to this concerto during this time, which may be described as the years in which he attempted to bring to a close his own personal period of *Sturm und Drang*. During the winters he spent in Detmold (1857, 1858 and 1859) he worked on the two Serenades for Orchestra (Op 11 and Op 16) and started writing *Lieder* (songs) again, such as 'Unter Blüten des Mai's spielt ich mit ihrer Hand'[99] (Beneath the blossom of May, I toyed with her hand). In this instance, the hand celebrated through Hölty's verses did actually exist; and Brahms actually toyed with it. The hand belonged to Agathe von Siebold, the daughter of a Göttingen doctor, who was not only young and pretty but also had a fine singing voice. Julius Otto Grimm, a good friend to Brahms ever since he first arrived in Düsseldorf, was director of music in Göttingen; it was in his house that Brahms met Agathe. The gentle encouragement that Grimm and his wife gave the relationship in the early days seems later to have turned into the well-intentioned mania that married couples often develop regarding matchmaking their unmarried friends. Initially, however, they saw themselves as a foursome, *a four-leaf clover*, as Brahms put it:

Now evening has come at last, or rather night has fallen. I'm alone and undisturbed and can write to you, dearest cloverleaf. –

There won't be much news. –

With me everything peters out in dashes –

Here is something else for you to comment on.

I must have the 'Bridal Song' back right away! . . . Without delay, please.

And with the Serenade and with his comments. Lengthy and precise ones. I'll overlook philistinism. I don't give a damn if none of the new pieces appeals to him one bit. In that case I shall turn to the fair sex, they don't ask for scores. There are a few songs on their way as well, in place of the letters I haven't time to write . . .

Give Agathe my greetings. I enclose a few songs for her which –

someone – well, and in doing so I wish, well – in brief, very politely for me.

And, Ise, don't be shy about pulling my things to pieces. A man who can be amusing can be forgiven much.

I do adore our cloverleaf four. But our letter-writing rather less. Such long rests, so few notes!

I hope to have my music back by Tuesday or Wednesday.

A thousand goodnights

and yet again

Your melancholy

Johannes. [100]

It is quite clear from this letter that Brahms was in love – *With me everything peters out in dashes.* Then he changes the subject and writes about his work in a jocular tone before turning to talk of Agathe with increasing incoherence. As we have seen from everything he said, Brahms was a man of conscience; for him being in love was no simple matter. He took it very seriously, even if in the broad daylight of Detmold, he appeared able to joke about it: *You've got a surprise coming! You* (he is speaking to a younger friend, Karl von Meysenburg) *go into raptures about the stiff ladies of the court here, but just you wait until you meet the beautiful, lively professors' daughters there* [in the university town of Göttingen]. [101] Brahms learnt how to put on a hearty front, which he later cultivated to the point of brusqueness and rudeness. But during the 'Agathe summer' of 1858, his true feelings could still be read clearly from his remarks, letters and, as always and best of all, his compositions. After all, he was only 25.

In order to understand Brahms's emotional state, the great joy with which he devoted himself to this love, the inner conflict and turmoil he had so recently left behind him must be borne in mind. He had accepted the renunciation of Clara Schumann, but ultimately he saw it as having been forced upon him. There were two insurmountable obstacles in the way of marriage between them. On the one hand, the shadow of Robert Schumann lay heavily on their relationship; on the other, Brahms knew that he had to free himself from the influence of a more mature woman whose artistic destiny was already fulfilled. It later became apparent that, for all the goodwill Clara had shown in trying to comprehend his music, she eventually capitulated in the face of his modernity.

So it is only against the background of his relationship with Clara that we can fully understand how Brahms responded, at first tentatively and then joyously, to the love Agathe proffered. It was a new feeling and he enjoyed it unreservedly, so unreservedly indeed, that when Clara came on a visit to Göttingen, she felt hurt and quickly left again. However, she had no real cause to feel hurt; the defining experience in Brahms's life was and would remain the 'Werther experience' he had shared with her. One of the finest and most touching aspects of Brahms's life is that his embattled relationship with Clara Schumann went on to develop into a friendship – if at times a difficult one – that only death could end. *If you think that the worst is to be expected send me word, so I can come and see those dear eyes still open; with them – how much will close for me,* Brahms wrote shortly before Clara's death in 1896.[102] He outlived her by less than a year.

On the other hand it was quite understandable that Clara Schumann did feel hurt during the 'Agathe summer' of 1858. It must have seemed that Brahms had found consolation inappropriately quickly. As it turned out, any consolation he enjoyed was evidently rather brief. Scarcely had the couple exchanged rings, than Brahms was seized with panic. He broke off the engagement. His letter to her speaks for itself; it is also consistent with his compulsion to evade settling down. *I love you! I must see you again! But I cannot be bound! Write and tell me if I should come again to enfold you in my arms, to kiss you, to tell you I love you!*[103] To the modern ear this might sound melodramatic, but at least it did express exactly the emotional contradiction that tormented him. Above all it was apparently effective. There was no confrontation with Agathe, but even Clara Schumann was concerned. 'I could not get poor Agathe and many other things out of my mind,' she wrote to him. 'I kept on seeing the poor, abandoned girl and lived through her sufferings with her. Oh, my dear Johannes, you shouldn't have let things go that far.'[104] Clara's sympathy is certainly genuine; she too had suffered, and was presumably still suffering from her separation from Brahms.

And what of Brahms? *I am in love with music, I love music, I think of nothing else, and only of other things when they make music more beautiful for me. I am composing love songs again, not addressed, let it be noted, to A-Z, but to music.*[105] This will have fooled nobody; some years later he even went so far as to create a public memorial to his love for Agathe von Siebold. The motif A-G-A-H(B natural)-E[106] appears in the subsidiary theme of the first movement of the famous and often quoted G major String Sextet Op 36, which he composed in 1864–65. He even revealed the connection to a friend, Josef Gänsbacher, at the time: *There I freed myself from my last love.*[107] It was not in fact to be his last love, but he did keep on 'freeing himself'. However, he never again let himself become quite as deeply involved as he had with Agathe von Siebold.

There may be more to the A-G-A-H-E motif than 'remembrance of times past'. In the tenth of the *12 Songs and Romances*, Op 44, published in 1861, the 'Agathe' motif appears as an ostinato figure in the alto line; the words it accompanies are:

> Und gehst du über den Kirchhof,
> da findest du ein frisches Grab;
> da senkten sie mit Tränen
> ein schönes Herz hinab.

Und fragst du, woran es gestorben,
kein Grabstein Antwort gibt;
doch flüstern leise die Winde:
es hatte zu heiß geliebt.

(And if you pass by the churchyard
You'll see a grave all fresh and new;
The tear-soaked earth there covers
A fair heart and a true.

And if you ask how it perished,
No gravestone's there to tell;
But the wind will softly whisper,
It loved, and loved too well.)[108]

Since leaving Hamburg in 1853, Brahms had only returned to the city of his birth intermittently, until the beginning of the period that could be called his 'Hamburg years', which ran from 1859 to 1862. A wedding initiated this period of activity in the city, though the couple themselves – a Pastor Sengelmann and Fräulein Jenny von Ahsen, whom Brahms had known for some time – had little to do with it. During the ceremony, Brahms's friend Karl G P Grädener performed a motet with his female pupils. This gave Brahms the idea of asking if he might perform his own *Ave Maria*, composed in Detmold in 1858, with the same group; the rehearsals for this piece led to the formation of a full-blown women's choir. *I am here, and presumably will stay here until I go to Detmold. A few very pleasant young ladies (pupils) keep me here and, in particular, a women's choir that sings under my direction, and so far only things I compose for them. I like their clear, silvery tones very much; the women's voices sound especially delightful in church accompanied by the organ.*[109]

In the *Avertimento*, the rules he drew up for the Hamburg Women's Choir in 1860, the serious Brahms even displayed a certain sense of humour. These rules include: *Primo: allow me to advise that the ladies of the choir must be present. Secundo* is the same, only with the rider that being present means being punctual. *Quarto* was clearly important to Brahms, as he got the choir to perform his own music: *be it noted that* [while] *the musical materials are largely entrusted to the discretion of the ladies, they must be guarded with all due care and attention by the aforementioned honourable and virtuous maidens and ladies and under no circumstances employed outside the Society.* The document is signed:

> *I remain,*
> *The Ladies of the Choir's most obedient, devoted,*
> *notable and metronomical servant*
>
> *Johannes Kreisler jun*
> *alias Brahms*[110]

The choir gave open-air performances in a large garden in Eppendorf, at that time still outside the city, and Brahms sometimes received presents from the ladies there. *I still remember my delighted surprise when I saw the memento from the Women's Choir, the writing set so charmingly concealed beneath flowers.*[111] Brahms was very receptive to the approval of 'his' ladies; after a few successful concerts there, his self-confidence had increased to the extent that he could even write to Clara Schumann about his *favourite pupil*, since this time there was not very much to it. He could also even write about tours of England in a relaxed, ironic tone; this had previously been a sore point, since it was her concert tours of England that had taken Clara away from him at the time when his passion for her had burnt most fiercely. His letters from Hamburg now strike quite a different note from the earlier correspondence:

My favourite pupil, Fräulein Wagner is here . . . She is an extremely charming, modest and musical girl, I'm sure you'd like her very much. She occasionally seems slightly standoffish, but it's easy to see through . . . she plays all sorts of things very prettily with her little fingers . . .

I don't think for a moment I shall ever go to England, at least not until I've walked all round Swabia and the magnificent German forests, not until I've been to the Tyrol, Switzerland, Italy, Greece, Egypt, India etc, etc, despite choirs of 3000 singing Handel and the magnificent scenery and battle scenes in Shakespeare's plays . . .[112]

These years were very stimulating for Brahms. His work with the choir, and occasionally the orchestra, in Detmold and with the Women's Choir, and the ladies' quartet that formed its nucleus, in Hamburg provided him with valuable opportunities to find out how his compositions worked in performance. Further stimulus came from his acquaintance with the *Lieder* singer Julius Stockhausen. Initially Stockhausen held Brahms in high regard as an accompanist; he later became the leading exponent of Brahms's songs. Brahms accompanied him in Beethoven *Lieder* and Schubert song cycles and was then inspired to try the genre himself. He found his text for the songs in the story of the love between Fair Magelone and the Count of Provence from *Phantasus* (1812–17), a mixture of poems, fairy tales and plays by the early Romantic writer Ludwig Tieck.

The 15 *Magelone Romanzen* Op 33 were written in Hamburg in 1861 and 1862. They are far from being imitation Schubert, but are as quintessentially Brahms as most of his works, including those clearly based on the forms of earlier composers. Max Kalbeck, Brahms's most important early biographer, writes in detail about the *Magelone* settings; his interpretation is very telling. 'The composer has saved all the concentrated power and sweetness of the vocal melody for the wonderful F sharp major passage, which links two of the poems. The anticipation and recollection of happiness combine in a feeling of plaintively transfigured joy . . . Here

Brahms comes close to Wagner. The magnificent A flat major passage in the second act of *Tristan*, "O sink hernieder, Nacht der Liebe" (O night of rapture rest upon us), can be heard in the distance "like the fleeting echo of a lute", as it says in *Magelone* – Isolde and Magelone exchanging sisterly greetings.'[113]

Friends were very important to Brahms. Like Goethe's Tasso, he believed that, 'Whoever cannot find a whole world in his friends, Does not deserve the world to hear of him.'[114] When he sent Joseph Joachim the score of his Second Serenade (Op 16), he wrote, *Look upon the piece with some affection, dear friend, it very much belongs to you; there is so much of you in it. After all, where does it come from when music has such a friendly ring if not from those few people one is as fond of as I am of you.*[115]

The baritone Julius Stockhausen (1826–1906) was catapulted to international fame after performing Mendelssohn's oratorio *Elijah* in Basle in 1848. He was particularly renowned for his interpretations of Schubert and Schumann, and toured extensively with Clara Schumann, Brahms and Joachim. He became music director of the Berlin Sternscher Gesangverein in 1874, and published his *Method of Singing* in 1887.

But it was also very important for Brahms that the wider world should 'hear of him'.

He was optimistic that he might find greater scope for his activities in Hamburg; after all, his B flat String Sextet Op 18 been performed there four times within a few weeks with great success. He wrote to several publishers, including Breitkopf & Härtel, to whom Robert Schumann had recommended him a few years earlier. But publishers are a cautious breed, and they had not forgotten the very public 'flop' of his First Piano Concerto in Leipzig. Consequently, of all the pieces Brahms offered them – the Piano Concerto, the two Serenades, the *Begräbnisgesang* (Funeral Hymn) and the *Ave Maria* – Breitkopf & Härtel took only the First Serenade in D major. However, the Swiss firm of Rieter-Biedermann in Winterthur did publish all of these works, as well as eight *Lieder und Romanzen* (*Songs and Romances*), in October 1860.

Earlier in 1860, Brahms had met the son of another music publisher at a commemoration for Robert Schumann. This would not have been a particularly noteworthy event, except that the son in question – Fritz Simrock (1838–1901) – was an exceptional publisher himself, who complemented his father's sure touch in contemporary music with a prescient eye for the musical direction of the future. He was an agreeable companion into the bargain, and Brahms got on well with him. Simrock immediately recognized Brahms's importance, much in the way that Schumann had done a decade earlier; he later became Brahms's publisher, but initially his father proceeded to publish his music with great caution. He took the Second Serenade, but other than that took only three pieces of chamber music between 1860 and 1867.

The difficulty that Brahms had in getting his works professionally published, even when he was relatively well known, would hardly be unfamiliar to a young composer today. Brahms's curmudgeonly attitude can not have helped: *I strongly beg you not to misinterpret the fact that I do not send you scores of my own music. The cause is my indecisiveness, the hope that I might send something better.*[116] Brahms knew that his music was considered 'difficult', and had hardly gained unqualified acceptance. So he was trying to change this perception when he wrote of some of his pieces, *They are very easy to perform and their effect has always, as for example in a public performance here, far exceeded my expectations . . .*[117] The great opportunity for music, the new 'market', that had opened up with its triumphal conquest of the middle-class drawing room, also had its downside: everything had to be as easy to play as possible. Even Beethoven had found himself reprimanded by his Scottish Publisher, G S Thomson, for making his piano parts too complex. Right until the end of his life Brahms was being urged by publishers to arrange all kinds of pieces for piano, two or four hands.

However, during the 'Hamburg years', at the beginning of the 1860s, Brahms was happy to see anything at all of his printed. His conflict with the Liszt school of 'New Germans', which dominated his life at this time, did not make things any easier for him. *I think my concerto is rather difficult to undertake. Added to that, almost all the competent pianists today belong to the New German School, which is perhaps not interested in my work.*[118] During these years, Brahms was very consciously fighting for recognition. In some of the things he said he occasionally sounds disheartened, . . . *but when you're approaching 30 and feel as weak as I do, then you're quite happy to shut yourself away in your room and stare at the walls in despondency,*[119] but his confidence in his own abilities was growing steadily stronger. In Hamburg he was unusually active; he gave piano lessons, rehearsed his choir, composed songs and chamber music, gave concerts, and even found time to pursue other hobbies. *I'm keeping at my gymnastic exercises and now I'm taking up Latin.*[120]

The experiences of the 'Düsseldorf years' had had a profound effect on Brahms, and the interlude of the 'Agathe summer' had probably come as a great relief. However, this was now all behind him, and he faced life with a freshness of vision and a new clarity of purpose. There is nothing final about these 'Hamburg years', they are more a period when he both collected himself and prepared the ground for his future development. With the advantage of hindsight, they can be seen as the years in which he lay the foundations for the second great encounter in his life. The first was with a woman, Clara Schumann, and the second would be with a city – Vienna. Prior to this great encounter, Brahms had assumed that he would be able to stay in Hamburg, where he had high hopes of being appointed conductor of the Philharmonic Society. However, this was not to be, and the disappointment of being passed over remained with him until late in life.

The 'Hamburg years' also brought wider recognition of Brahms's talent; something which he himself had been sure of for a long time. Even towards the end of 1859 he could write: *. . . I don't mind saying that I am very much pleased with my things. I really do think, dear Clara, that I'm growing!*[121] However, despite the calls for the composer after some concerts, which Brahms mentions in his letters, acclaim still came mostly from the circle of friends who understood his priorities. This can be seen in the comments Clara Schumann wrote in her diary for November and December 1861: 'Rehearsal of Johannes's G minor Quartet [Piano Quartet Op 25]. 16 November: soirée at my apartment. I was dreadfully nervous; it must have been my fear for the quartet, which I so very much wanted to be a success. However much I threw myself into it with all my love, the gentlemen scratched away or slept. The last movement made a big impression . . . December . . . On the 3rd I played Johannes's D minor Concerto with the Hamburg Philharmonic, which he conducted; I think I must have been the happiest person in the whole concert hall, for both the effort required by the demanding nature of the work and my own fear were outweighed by my pleasure in the piece and the fact that he himself was conducting, nothing else bothered me, not even the stupid audience – they understood nothing and felt nothing, otherwise they would at least have shown due respect, at least given the composer some sign of their sympathy – after all he is a child of this city [Hamburg]!'[122]

Indeed Brahms not only came from the city of Hamburg, he

was also very fond of it: *I'm a Hamburger through and through* he wrote to Joachim in 1859, even though he no longer felt quite at home living with his parents: *I do have one complaint. Living here gives me as much privacy as a servant with his bed in the kitchen.*[123] The composer Albert Dietrich gives us a picture of Brahms and his parents during these Hamburg years in his description of a visit to stay with them:

'In order to be able to work in peace, Brahms himself had a very pleasant flat in the suburb of Hamm . . . Contrary to his normal habit, he played some of his sketches to me[124] . . . I slept in his room and found it very interesting. I was astonished at his large library, which he had been busily collecting since he was a boy. Part of it he had bought on the bridges in the city where the booksellers set up their stalls . . . In the mornings I took my breakfast with his dear mother who, for all her simplicity, was a woman of great tact and sensitivity . . . His father usually left at an early hour for his work as a double-bass player and music teacher. One day I visited Brahms in his delightful garden flat, where we spent the time looking through his latest works . . . A musical highlight of those days was a charming *ladies'* quartet who performed four-part songs by Brahms to us quite beautifully in the neighbouring garden.'[125]

Here we have all the component elements of Brahms's Hamburg environment: his parents, his ladies' quartet (obviously the nucleus of the chamber choir) and the space he always needed 'in order to be able to work in peace' once he had taken his musical ideas for a 'long enough walk'.

Brahms composed two important sets of variations during these 'Hamburg years': the Variations on a Theme by Schumann Op 23 and the Variations and Fugue on a Theme by Handel Op 24. As Brahms moved towards the challenge of symphonic writing, the 'giant footsteps' that he heard behind him were not only those of Beethoven, but also of Bach. The *Handel Variations* were

Brahms's highly successful attempt to match the enormous structural, aesthetic and emotional challenge of Bach's *Goldberg Variations*. This work was among his favourite from the past, and at his death, it was Bach's picture that was hanging over his bed. In February 1865, Josef Gänsbacher found his friend Brahms, just after he had been told that his mother was dying, '. . . playing the Bach variations with tears running down his cheeks. He didn't stop when I came in, but just said, *They're like balm.*'[126]

These two sets of keyboard variations, in which his relationship to the musical tradition and canon is more openly stated by Brahms than in any other genre, are excellent illustrations of his powers of assimilation. He called the *Handel Variations* his *favourite work*. Once again, he had to fight to get it printed, writing to Breitkopf & Härtel: *I am unwilling, at the first hurdle, to give up my desire to see this, my favourite work, published by you. If, therefore, it is primarily the high fee that stops you taking it, I will be happy to let you have it for 12 Friedrichsdors or, if this still seems too high, 10 Friedrichsdors.*

I very much hope you will not think I plucked the initial fee arbitrarily out of the air.

I consider this work to be much better than my earlier ones; I think it is also better adapted to the demands of performance and will therefore be easier to market . . .[127]

By this time Brahms had acquired a degree of financial security. His appearances as a piano soloist brought in a tidy sum and, given his thrift, there was always some of it

Felix Mendelssohn (1809–47) was encouraged by his teacher Carl Friedrich Zelter to study Bach, who, despite the efforts of late-18th-century enthusiasts, such as the Baron von Swieten and Nicolaus Forkel, was known for only a handful of his works. In 1829, the 20-year-old composer conducted Bach's *Matthew Passion* at the Berlin *Singakademie*, the first performance since the death of Bach. In Mendelssohn's own words, 'it was an actor and a Jew who restored this great Christian work to the people'. In 1840, he organized the erection of a statue of Bach outside the Thomaskirche in Leipzig.

left. But he didn't sit on it, as can be seen in the well-known anecdote about his departure from Hamburg: '*Father*, he said with a roguish smile as he took his leave, *if things get bad you'll find the best consolation is in music. Have a good look at my old copy of* Saul *and you'll find what you're looking for.* He had stuffed the volume full of banknotes.'[128]

On 8 September 1862 Brahms went to Vienna for the first time. The visit was primarily arranged because the committee of the Hamburg Philharmonic Society had cautiously suggested that he should, if possible, not go too far away from that city, so that they could 'bring him back' if necessary. On arriving in Vienna, however, he learnt to his horror that the position that he had sought as conductor of the society had been offered to the singer Julius Stockhausen, who had next to no orchestral experience. Brahms could be forgiven for wondering if this decision had more to do with class than ability.

One of the first letters Brahms wrote after his arrival in Vienna exclaims *Yes, that's how it is! I have stirred my stumps and I'm living here, a stone's throw from the Prater, and I can drink my wine where Beethoven drank his.*[129] Hardly had Brahms arrived than the first label was attached to him. Usually, the more grandiose the label imposed on Brahms, the more deadly the effect it had on his contemporaries. In this case, however, it was its originator rather than the composer himself who later found it exceptionally embarrassing, especially after he had joined the 'opposing camp'. Vienna easily merits being described as music's capital during this period; it could equally be called the capital of musical intrigue and faction. In due course Brahms himself would learn this painful lesson.

The label that was attached to Brahms during that first stay in Vienna was the result of his visit to the house of the pianist Julius Epstein, to whom he had an introduction, in October 1862. Josef Hellmesberger, the leader of the Philharmonic Orchestra, was playing Brahms's G minor Piano Quartet Op 25 with him at sight (Brahms made his Vienna debut with this piece, playing with Hellmesberger's group, a few weeks later); and when they had finished, he exclaimed, 'This is Beethoven's heir!'[130] Obviously it was said in the heat of the moment, but it proved prescient. Hellmesberger later excused himself by saying he had drunk too much wine, but he had no need, for it is in his chamber music above all that Brahms most justifies the moniker of 'Beethoven's heir'. For while his symphonic work actively quotes Beethoven, his chamber music actually carries on from where the late Beethoven quartets had left off.

Hellmesberger's remark also had a specifically Viennese resonance. For the house in which it was made was the one in which Mozart lived from 1784–7, and where he composed *The Marriage of Figaro*, the Masonic Funeral Music and the D minor Piano Concerto K 466, which Brahms had often performed. It was also at this house that Haydn played the string quartets Mozart had dedicated to him, and where Beethoven was said to have played for Mozart on his first visit to Vienna in 1787.

Brahms was given a warm and friendly welcome on his first stay in Vienna. Of course at this stage, no one yet regarded him as a rival. Almost against his will, or at least not at his instigation, concerts of his music were immediately organized. The first, following on from the sight-reading session with Hellmesberger, took place on 16 November in the concert hall of the *Musikverein*, where his G minor Piano Quartet was included in one of the Hellmesberger Quartet's regular concerts. This was followed on 29 November by a concert in which Brahms appeared as pianist; the programme included his enigmatic Piano Quartet in A major Op 26, the Variations and Fugue on a Theme by Handel Op 24, Bach's F major Toccata for Organ and Schumann's C major Fantasy Op 17.

Yesterday brought me great joy, Brahms wrote to his parents, *my concert went quite splendidly, much better than I had hoped.*

After my quartet had been favourably received, my solo playing was a great success with the audience. Every piece was most warmly applauded; I believe there was real enthusiasm in the hall . . .

I played as freely as if I'd been at home with friends – but of course this audience stimulates you very differently from ours.

You should see how attentive they are and hear their applause![131]

Soon after his arrival in the city, Brahms discovered Viennese popular music. He fell in love with it on the spot, and it became a lifelong passion. At that time there were 'flying' bands in Vienna that went from one tavern to another and Brahms was particularly fond of them, as he was of the Hungarian Ladies' Band in the Prater park. He was also soon introduced to the grander echelons of Viennese society. He gave piano lessons and got to know a number of musicians who quickly became friends. Among the first of these were the singing teacher Josef Gänsbacher and the pianist Carl Tausig. 'Brahms was a frequent self-invited guest to Tausig's fashionable apartment in

The 'Musikverein' was completed in 1869 as the concert hall of Vienna's Gesellschaft der Musikfreunde. This society of the friends of music had, up until this point, been giving its concerts in the Redoutensaal of the Imperial Palace. The interior of the new hall was encrusted with fabulous golden biscuit work designed by the painter Hans Makart. The small hall, which was inaugurated with a recital by Clara Schumann in 1870, is today called the Brahmssaal. Ironically, Brahms himself never liked the acoustic there.

Währinger Strasse . . . playing four-handed pieces with him, lying on his sofa, enjoying his oldest brandy and newest dirty jokes, smoking Turkish tobacco and being initiated by Tausig into the mysteries of Schopenhauer's philosophy.'[132]

Although Vienna accorded its new resident a generous welcome, at this stage Brahms could hardly have guessed that he was going to become Viennese by adoption. His mind was still very much on Hamburg, and when the news arrived that the completely inexperienced Julius Stockhausen had been appointed conductor of the Hamburg Philharmonic over him, he was profoundly hurt. 'The history of music will not forget the wrong done to Johannes,'[133] Joachim wrote in high dudgeon to a member of the Philharmonic committee. Brahms himself wrote to Clara Schumann, *For me it is a much sadder event than you may think or perhaps find conceivable . . . I am a rather old-fashioned person, old-fashioned amongst other things in that I am not cosmopolitan, but am attached to my native city as to a mother . . . Now this unfriendly friend comes along and pushes me out – for ever, I suppose. How seldom does someone like us find a fixed abode, how I would have liked to find one in my native city. Now, here, where there is so much to delight me, I nevertheless feel, and will always feel, that I am a stranger and cannot find peace.*[134]

Carl Tausig (1841–71) became Liszt's student at the age of 14; and his teacher described him as having 'fingers of steel'. He made his debut under von Bülow in 1858 in Berlin, toured extensively and was principally known for his spectacular technical feats. Brahms's studies with him resulted in his somewhat atypically virtuoso *Paganini Variations* Op 35. Tausig's *Daily Studies* are still seen as indispensable by many pianists. He died of typhus.

Yet for all his complaining, Brahms accepted this effective banishment at once. This was typical of the simultaneous search for and flight from security that is such an important motif in Brahms's life. His independent existence was a source of suffering for him, yet he clung onto it desperately. Had he been truly Bohemian at heart rather than a solid citizen, he would have been quite happy to content himself with Tausig's brandy, his crush on the Vienna 'Fidelio', the singer Luise Dunstmann, and with writing transcendental virtuoso works such as the *Paganini Variations*, which had its origin in the enjoyment Brahms derived from playing with Tausig.

But Brahms was no Bohemian; he went back to Hamburg. *I am old-fashioned enough to suffer from homesickness, and so I shall probably leave here when spring is at its loveliest, to go and see my old mother.*[135] His parents were squabbling at this time, and ultimately separated. Brahms could not settle their differences, but he could at least give them financial assistance. In the meantime, he stayed in Blankenese, a pleasant suburb on the Elbe, where he composed the cantata *Rinaldo* Op 50. He originally intended to enter this piece in a competition organized by the Aachen choral society, the 'Liedertafel'. Such competitions were very characteristic of this period, when artistic production was very much dominated by the middle classes. Unlike Beethoven, the generation of musicians to which Brahms belonged had no need of patrons such as Prince Lichnowsky, patronage of the arts having largely passed to the bourgeoisie.

Brahms was still in Blankenese when he received the offer to become the conductor of the *Singakademie*, a Viennese choral society. This he accepted, albeit with a degree of trepidation. *It's just that it is a very special decision to give up one's freedom for the first time.* But there was one thing Brahms now knew for sure: *However, anything that comes from Vienna sounds all the more beautiful to a musician, and anything that calls him there is all the more enticing.*[136] When Brahms accepted the post he probably did not know that he had been chosen by the smallest possible majority (39 votes to 38), nor did he know how difficult the choir's situation was. It had been founded in 1858 in protest against the *Gesellschaft der Musikfreunde* doing so little for choral music; the *Gesellschaft der Musikfreunde* immediately countered this by setting up its own choir, the *Singverein*, under the brilliant conductor Johann von Herbeck.

Brahms, as Beckerath's drawings indicate, was far from being a brilliant conductor. He often kept one hand in his pocket, although this was far from unusual in the 19th century. 'I am sure he "conducted to himself", just as he played to himself.'[137] The first rehearsals with the new choir in Vienna took place at the end of September 1863. On the way there, Brahms stayed in Baden-Baden, where Clara Schumann was spending the summer. There he met the Russian pianist and composer Anton Rubinstein and the writer Ivan Turgenev, who later tried to offer him stories for operas. The King and Queen of Prussia and Bismarck were also in Baden-Baden at the time, though presumably Brahms only saw them from a distance.

Back in Vienna, Brahms threw himself into his work as choirmaster. Initially, the members of the choir were full of curiosity about their new conductor and very ready to respond. However, their attention soon began to slacken and Brahms, who had already been criticized for his excessive fondness for Bach, found it difficult to get his ideas accepted. Some members stopped coming to rehearsals, and by the time he gave his second concert it was 'more of an improvisation or choir practice than a public performance.'[138] Yet when the time for re-election came, Brahms was unanimously re-elected director of the *Singakademie*. At first he hesitated, then accepted, but finally withdrew. He never really enjoyed the position, not

Brahms, the conductor. Drawing by W von Beckerath

because it was a 'position', but because of the practical difficulties. It was certainly not that he lacked talent as a teacher; reports of his piano lessons and descriptions of his work with the Hamburg ladies' choir show that he was a gifted motivator.

Florence May, an English woman who first met Brahms during a summer stay in Baden-Baden in 1871, wrote a pen portrait of him at the time. She would later contribute the first major biography of the composer in English. 'Brahms, then, when I first knew him was in the very prime of life, being 38 years of age. Below middle height, his figure was somewhat square and solidly built, though without any of the tendency to corpulence which developed itself at a later period. He was of the blonde type of German, with fair, straight hair, which he wore rather long and brushed back from the temples. His face was clean-shaven. His most striking characteristic was the grand head with its magnificent intellectual forehead . . . In Brahms's demeanour there was a mixture of sociability and reserve . . .'[139] This is Brahms in his 'middle' years. One thing that particularly impressed Florence May was the way in which, when playing four-handed pieces with Clara Schumann, Brahms was 'always allowed to retain the beloved cigar or cigarette between his lips during the performance'.[140]

As a piano teacher he was 'strict and absolute; he was gentle and patient and encouraging; he was not only clear, he was light itself; he knew exhaustively, and could teach, and did teach, by the shortest possible methods, every detail of technical study . . . He was never irritable, never indifferent, but always helped, stimulated and encouraged. One day, I lamented to him the deficiencies of my former mechanical training and my present resultant finger difficulty, *It will come all right,* he said; *it does not come in a week nor in four weeks . . .* He loved Bach's suspensions. *It is here that it must sound*, he would say, pointing to the tied note, and insisting, whilst not allowing me to force the

Brahms in 1875

preparation, that the latter should be so struck as to give the fullest possible effect to the dissonance. "How am I to make this sound?" I asked him of a few bars of subject lying for the third, fourth and fifth fingers of the left hand, which he wished brought out clearly, but in a very soft tone. *You must think particularly of the fingers with which you play it, and by and by it will come out*, he answered.'[141]

This extract reveals far more of Brahms than merely his teaching methods. However, the attention to practical detail that May describes only really takes on significance as a characteristic of Brahms the musician when seen in conjunction with a further remark typical of his understanding of music. '"All that you have told me today,"' she said to him after her first Mozart lesson, '"is quite new to me." *It's all there,* he replied, pointing to the music.'[142]

Brahms also gave piano lessons in Vienna, after he had given up being a choirmaster there. His female pupils became acolytes and admirers, sometimes lifelong friends, although usually, as in the case of his 'soul mate' Elisabet von Stockhausen, later von Herzogenberg, only after they were married.

Brahms also spent time in Vienna researching the neglected music of Schubert:

In fact, my best hours here are spent with unpublished works by Schubert; I have the manuscripts of quite a few in my apartment. But however delightful and enjoyable studying them is, almost everything else about them is just sad. For example, I have many things here in

manuscript which belong to Spina or Schneider of which only the man-
uscript exists, nothing else, not one single copy! And Spina no more keeps
his things in a fireproof safe than I do.

Recently a whole pile of unpublished things was offered for sale at
an unbelievably low price, but fortunately they were acquired by the
Gesellschaft der Musikfreunde. How many other things are scattered here
and there in the possession of private individuals who either guard their
treasure like dragons or carelessly allow them to disappear.[143]

This would not be the sole musicological task that Brahms
undertook. He not only studied the techniques of older music,
but did much to preserve and edit the works of earlier composers.
He made his attitude to his great predecessors clear, for instance
at a wine-tasting that he attended in 1876. The finest of the
wines tasted was a '56 Rauentaler. One of the 'culture-vulture'
businessmen attending declared, 'What Brahms is among composers, this '56 Rauentaler is among Rhine wines!' To which
Brahms is said to have replied, *Then give us a bottle of old Bach.*[144]
Brahms also took on the editing of Mozart's *Requiem* for Breitkopf
& Härtel's 'critical edition'.

When his friend, the critic Eduard Hanslick, sent him two
early works by Beethoven that had been thought lost, despite his
increasing reluctance to write letters as he got older, Brahms's
pen ran away with him:

Dear friend,

You've gone away and left me a treasure . . . Even without seeing
the name on the title page one could not have come up with any other –
it is Beethoven through and through. The beauty and nobility of emo-
tion, the magnificence of feeling and imagination, the power – even ferocity
– of expression, the handling of the parts, the declamation, and in the
last two aspects all the characteristics we observe and ponder in his later
works . . .[145]

A constant theme that emerges from Brahms's work on earlier
composers is his concern at the possible loss of great works from

the past. The fear that masterpieces might be lost to music became much stronger in the 19th century than in the 18th century, when the interest in 'ancient' music was only in its infancy. In this Brahms was following in the footsteps of Mendelssohn, who practically single-handedly spearheaded the revival of Bach. However, Brahms's interest was not a populist one. It seems to have been a matter of secondary importance to him that these works from the past be made available to the general public; on the contrary, he was not entirely in favour of the flood of publications:

Publishing has now become so much the fashion, particularly the publishing of things that don't warrant it at all.

You know my old pet wish, that the so-called works of the masters – even those of the great ones, and certainly those of the lesser ones – should not be published too completely, but that good copies, and copies of genuinely complete works, should be lodged in the major libraries.[146]

Brahms, a 'child of his time' in this too, was no populist. He saw only that the works of the great masters needed preserving, and that he, whose approach was based entirely upon them, and a few others who understood them, might need access to them. What was Brahms's relationship to the fragments of older music and conventions that he increasingly referenced in his compositions? His work was certainly far beyond mere imitation, or of pastiche.

The critic Eduard Hanslick (1825–1904), a supporter of Brahms and a fanatical opponent of Wagner, made an error in his assessment of Brahms that was to have far-reaching consequences. (His anti-Wagner stance did bring him lasting fame, however, when Wagner immortalized him as Beckmesser in *Die Meistersinger von Nürnberg*; even in the draft version of the list of characters he is still called 'Veit Hanslich, scribe'.) Hanslick's error was to see Brahms as the leader of a movement. As an artist, Brahms was clearly so insular and so introverted that the last thing he would do would be to establish a 'school'. On top of this, he and his music looked back to the past. There was no other composer, far and wide, who produced so little that was obviously 'new' and yet so much that was original and individual. The 'Brahmins', Hanslick's own invention, were followers and admirers; they were not, and never became, a new school. Eduard Hanslick played an important role in Brahms's life. However, his aggressive sympathy for Brahms was probably as much a product of his aggressive antipathy to Wagner as of any profound understanding of Brahms's music. But perhaps such an absolute categorization does him an injustice. He was in fact rather difficult to pin down, and Brahms himself does not make it any easier for us. *I do not think Hanslick ever had any real feeling for my music,*[147] he said, before making the admission that implicitly accepts Hanslick's lack of understanding of his music: *I cannot help it,* he wrote to Clara Schumann, *but I know few people towards whom I feel as warmly as I do towards him. To be so artless, good, benevolent, honest,*

Hanslick worships at the altar of Brahms. A contemporary caricature

earnest, modest and whatever as I know him to be, seems to me something very beautiful and very rare.[148]

Hanslick was not only a critic, he was the first to occupy the chair of The Aesthetics and History of Music at the University of Vienna; he was involved when Brahms took up an appointment in the city for the second time. In the autumn of 1872 Brahms was made musical director of the *Gesellschaft der Musikfreunde* and of its choir, the *Singverein*, a move to the opposite

The Czech-born critic Eduard Hanslick (1825–1904) did more than any other writer to further the dispute as to the nature of true German music in the second half of the 19th century. A virulent opponent of the Liszt–Wagner movement, he was one of the earliest supporters of Schumann. His review of Adolf Brodsky's premiere of the Tchaikovsky violin concerto is legendary: 'The violin is no longer played . . . it is yanked about . . . beaten black and blue.'

faction to the one that had first provided him with employment in that city.

His apartment at that time was in Karlsgasse, across the square from the Musikverein. The apartment building no longer exists, but the Musikverein looks just as it did in Brahms's day; and this is where his statue now stands. Looking out of the windows of the Musikverein across the square to the Karlskirche (whose architecture Brahms loved), gives a good sense of the feeling of the place in the 1870s.

As musical director of the *Musikfreunde*, Brahms insisted on going his own way. Hanslick, who was the most sophisticated of Brahms's admirers, if also slightly superficial, typically still manages to make a joke of his irritation at Brahms's independence. 'There is in Vienna', he wrote following the Gesellschaft der Musikfreunde concert of 6 April 1873, at which Brahms conducted Bach's cantata *Liebster Gott, wann werd ich sterben* and Cherubini's *Requiem*, 'an audience for music that is serious as well as beautiful, but nobody here goes to a concert with the sole purpose of being buried twice, first according to the Protestant rite, and then to the Catholic, anymore than they do anywhere else.'[149]

Brahms at home in Vienna

Brahms overdid the earnestness, perhaps out of a part-conscious, part-subconscious compulsion to use it as an antidote to the cosily familiar, a rejection of a certain Viennese *Gemüt-lichkeit*. It would be simplifying things too much to characterize him as sombre. After all, he did choose to stay in Vienna, or to return constantly to that city, because he felt that its blend of light-heartedness and darker undertones, which came from an awareness of transience, corresponded to his own feelings about life. Yet his reluctance to 'sing his heart out' remained, and sensitive friends pointed this out. 'And are you not sorry you were in such haste to repent your display of emotion?'[150] wrote Elisabet von Herzogenberg in a long letter to Brahms regarding his Fourth Symphony Op 98, in 1885.

Elisabet von Herzogenberg (1847–92), Brahms's 'soul mate', was the wife of Freiherr Heinrich von Herzogenberg, who had given up a career in law to devote himself to music. He studied with Otto Dessoff, conductor of the Court Opera in Vienna and director of the Philharmonic concerts, and Brahms had a high opinion of him. However, he was irritated when people compared Herzogenberg's compositions to his own.

In one such case Elisabet made no secret of *her* anger. Not mincing her words, she rebuked Brahms, the friend she respected and admired, for giving vent to his wounded pride when a critic, who had dismissed his B flat major String Quartet Op 67 'with disdain', praised a quartet by Herzogenberg that was played during the same season. Brahms had recounted all this to her husband, wrote Elisabet 'with a certain complacent irony, as if to say: Of course the man has made a fool of himself for all time,' and went on, 'Now it was no impartial third party to whom you were speaking, but to the one man you know to be the first to laugh at such an ignoramus; no puffed-up creature just asking to be cured of his high opinion of himself, but one who does not think himself worthy to untie your shoes.'

Austrian pianist Elisabet von Herzogenberg: *one had no choice but to fall in love with her*

Elisabet was ready to speak her mind. She was addressing a problem experienced by all those who felt close to Brahms, not least Clara Schumann: the wounding brusqueness with which the lonely Brahms made himself even lonelier. 'I know you don't mean to be cruel,' Elisabet continued, 'but at such moments you seem to have a fiend on your back (not a regular companion, thank God!) prompting remarks that are deadly in their power to wound others. If you only knew how deadly they are, you would give them up for good.'[151] But Brahms could not give them up, for his brusqueness was the unavoidable flipside of his sensitivity and his inability to 'open up' fully to other people.

When, at the age of 30, he composed his first song cycle, the *Lieder und Gesänge* Op 32, published in 1864, the 'inhibiting shackle' in the fifth poem of the set must have sounded very familiar to him: 'Alas, do you come once more to clasp me, inhibiting shackle? Up and away into the air.' And the poem ends: 'Exhale the foe from your breast.' The poet could 'exhale the foe' in his poetry alone: 'Let the soul's longing flow, flow into clamorous songs,' and in the same way Brahms could only really shed the 'inhibiting shackle' through his music. He found company difficult. He could be merry, though his humour tended to be rather strained, and could be a strain on his listeners too, especially when he was teasing. At any rate, people were glad when Brahms was happy; his bad moods could paralyse a gathering in no time at all. The older he became, the less he was willing to open up and reveal his feelings. He said nothing, but expected to be understood.

Elisabet von Herzogenberg was a gifted pianist. 'I was delighted at her talent and amazed at her progress. She had the softest touch, the most fluent technique, the quickest grasp, the most unusual memory and the most expressive playing – in a word she was a genius. At the same time she was very beautiful, intelligent, cultured, noble and enchantingly charming. One had no choice but to fall in love with her.'[152] There is only one thing to add to this portrayal of Elisabet by her teacher Julius Epstein: Brahms did indeed fall in love with her. This happened when he met up with her again in 1874, on his first return to Leipzig after the failure of his *Requiem* there in 1869 (by the audience that had rejected his First Piano Concerto ten years earlier). Now that his former pupil was married, he could safely fall in love with her without risking his precious freedom unfettered by family ties. This love then developed into a new kind of relationship with a woman, one based on a warmth of understanding unclouded by physical desire, which focused above all on his work. 'You know the delight with which we in the Humboldtstrasse hail every shaving from your workshop.'[153]

We are able to draw a picture of Brahms's feelings and attitudes through the people who were close to him because he lived out his life almost entirely within a restricted circle. There are few other artists for whom it would be more inappropriate to talk about their public. Brahms, an individualist, was dependent on other individuals. The fame his music eventually brought made him no less gruffly uncommunicative, no less shy; the recognition he sought came from individual people.

My most honoured and dear, or most dear and honoured friend, he wrote to Elisabet von Herzogenberg, *I must confess, though with some constraint, that your letter was a real relief, for I was beginning*

*to think you had some grievance against me. Apparently not? And as
you yourself call me a good sort, and I can vouch for it being the case,
I beg to suggest that it is a pity to drift apart on account of minor matters. We meet with little enough that is good and few enough of the good
sort in this life.*

*Therefore I thank you again, most sincerely, for the tonic your kind
letter proved to be. And please don't suppress any nice things you have
to say about my music. It's good to be flattered now and then, most people
remain dumb until they find something to moan about.*[154]

So at the age of 46 he was still writing with youthful temerity;
even nine years later, in 1888, he is still wary: *Once more my most
sincere thanks, and if you should have sweetened the last letter too much
out of sheer kindness, I expect the bitter pill to follow to your Joh Br.*[155]

What is quite clear from this is that Brahms's success and
comfortable position had not gone to his head. His concert tours
had long been successful. By 1879, when the first of the two letters above was written, his First and Second Symphonies, Violin
Concerto, Third Piano Quartet and Third String Quartet had
already been performed. By this time he had also weathered the
huge success and equally huge scandal over his *Hungarian Dances*
WoO 1, his first truly popular work. Max Kalbeck described the
affair in his wistful and sententious manner: 'It was neither his
deeply expressive songs, nor his profound chamber music suffused with sweet melody that made Brahms really popular, but
his arrangement of the *Hungarian Dances*. Those who did not
know the name of Brahms – and how relatively few knew it in
1869! – now heard it in connection with that work. No wonder
that afterwards the leader of every gypsy band claimed to be the
originator of the *Hungarian Dances,* and cheated out of his
birthright.'[156]

However, the main focus of the scandal was on Brahms's
touring partner from back in 1853, the virtuoso violinist Ede
Reményi. Reményi publicly accused Brahms of robbing him of

the dances. The accusation caused an extraordinary stir. Brahms's friend Joachim wrote, 'The accusations concerning his *Hungarian Dances* are quite childish and ridiculous. Firstly Brahms specifically wrote *arranged* on the title page, and then they're generally known, that is, they are common property. Brahms certainly got some from Reményi. When they visited me in 1853 they were both enthusiastic about Hungarian music, as they were about all kinds of folk songs. But Brahms was such an industrious collector and possessed such extensive knowledge, that the aid of that imprecise Magyar was by no means essential. Some in the third and fourth volume are of Brahms's own invention, in fact he included these at the request of his publisher, to give them better protection against unauthorized copies of his arrangements; Nos 11, 14 and 16 I consider original Brahms.'[157] Of course, Joachim himself could hardly claim to be a disinterested party, as he had profitably arranged the dances for piano and violin, so as to play them himself; the disavowal of his rival Reményi's contribution to the pieces was hardly surprising.

In itself the story would be of no great importance, were it not for Brahms's own behaviour in the matter, which throws some light on his general attitude and outlook. Despite being at the centre of this scandal, he seemed almost completely untouched by it. He did say, *I couldn't learn the right things from Reményi, he brought too much untruth into them,*[158] but his real answer was to produce two new volumes of *Hungarian Dances,* which he published in 1880. They are, as he said of the first volumes, *genuine gypsy children, therefore not my offspring, just brought up by me on my own blood and milk.*[159]

Brahms was 'by nature incapable of carefree, much less of frivolous behaviour; he was not one of those men who will light their cigar from the sanctuary lamp.'[160] Nonetheless, he had developed a strength of character, a clarity, which did have something 'classical' about it and which can definitely be found in his music.

Brahms had come to decisions about his life. These had not appeared overnight; they had matured in his new environment and in the growing recognition his work enjoyed. Brahms had freed himself from Clara Schumann, from Agathe von Siebold and even, by this time, from any thought of sharing his life with another; he had left Hamburg and made a conscious decision to move to Vienna. In a letter to his father in 1869, he writes:

I keep thinking how I would like to be at home with you – but in the end it just isn't possible. To gratify this pet notion of mine, I've spent this last winter in a room at the inn. I have none of my books and scores with me and when I think about it seriously, I realize I don't need them in Hamburg. I really must make up my mind to live here; I must finally make up my mind to pay the rent where I intend to live . . .

Beside that, and in the long run, what is there for me to do in Hamburg? Apart from you, who is there I still want to see there? Etc, etc. You yourself know very well there's nothing there for me, not in any respect.

In short, I've finally come to realize I must be at home somewhere, . . . and so I've decided that in the autumn I'm going to make myself a little more comfortable here in Vienna. [161]

Alongside this final cutting of the umbilical cord with Hamburg came a further development in Brahms's life, a growing sense of being recognized as a composer at last. This new confidence was hard on the heels of the enthusiastic reception accorded the *German Requiem* Op 45 at its premiere in Bremen on Good Friday, 1868. Brahms himself had initially had some qualms about the *Requiem*: *My piece is quite difficult and in Bremen they are more cautious about going up to top 'A' than in Vienna etc.* [162]

He was also becoming financially independent, something that gave him even greater freedom and confidence. *I really would seriously like to send you some music soon. Unfortunately I am half performer, half composer. Only one who ate his bread with tears,* he wrote, misquoting the Harper in Goethe's *Wilhelm Meisters Lehrjahre, knows what it means to have the right music on his piano at the moment.*[163] He now earned enough as a pianist and conductor not to have to rely on what he could earn from publishers to pay the rent. He was already in a position to demand substantial fees. But it was not his life as a semi-performer that was an obstacle to his composing, it was simply that he didn't like writing quickly, and certainly not under onerous pressure from people or deadlines.

Brahms's reluctance to rush his composing led to a certain amount of friction with Fritz Simrock, who had taken over the publishing firm after his father's death and wanted to be *the* Brahms publisher. Simrock kept on pestering Brahms: 'Aren't you doing anything at all? Am I not going to get a symphony from you this year either?' he wrote in 1873. 'And the quartets and all the other things you keep in such short supply?'[164]

The money question bothered Brahms precisely because it was not important for him. For example, his publisher earned a fortune from his *Hungarian Dances,* while Brahms only received a one-off payment in addition to a second voluntary remuneration. It wasn't his publishers' earnings that irritated him, but the system of the one-off fee. He referred to it thus: *the confounded money relationship that is unfortunately still customary between musicians and publishers. We musicians are treated like children who can't understand their own affairs, we haven't the least idea what and how we're actually being paid, whether we're giving or getting, robbing or are being robbed.*[165] Brahms clearly was well aware of this particular problem; but in general he was not concerned with matters of principle. *Once something has three noughts at the end I'm happy with it. I'm not too concerned about the number in front.*[166] He could afford not to be too concerned; by this time everything he offered was not only printed, but he was well paid for it too. Occasionally, however, even he, who for the most part lived a self-contained life, became aware of the significance a change in payment terms from a one-off fee to a royalty would have for composers in general: *But it is not right that, with the popularity I enjoy, I have not pushed this change through. I am too impractical, too lazy, and too indecisive – and, given my sad solo situation, not personally interested – but it's still not right.*[167]

Although Brahms may at times have found him to be a pest, Fritz Simrock was just the type of publisher he needed to make his music widely known. In his way Simrock was certainly part of Brahms's close circle of friends, and Brahms was a frequent guest in his house. As a publisher he made a major contribution to the history of music by his early and unwavering commitment to Brahms.[168]

Another important figure in Brahms's life was the conductor Hans von Bülow. In some respects, Bülow looks somewhat out of place in the ranks of the friends who, together with his music, made up Brahms's life. Bülow was completely unlike Brahms in both appearance and temperament; indeed, he was his exact opposite. He was 'small, delicate, nimble, a bundle of nerves, with mordant wit, bubbling over with enthusiasm and malice. With his sparse, straight grey hair, his fine brow, smooth, but often furrowed with displeasure, his strikingly small, grey-blue eyes and sarcastic lips, the mocking expression on which was only intensified by his little moustache and stiletto beard, the sprightly little man was awhirl with vivacity.'[169] There was also a whiff of scandal about Bülow's support for Brahms. He had been a Wagnerian, indeed one of the most committed, but had defected, and his defection was certainly not unconnected with the fact that his wife had left him for Wagner. *The experience of his marriage,* Brahms once said, *made him unhappy. As did his relationship with Liszt. He was absolutely devoted to him and tried to make as much as possible of his compositions; eventually, however, he came to see that there was nothing to them. He once said to me, 'I have to keep myself so occupied, in such a state of excitement, all the time. I've been through such painful things, the mere memory could kill me.'*[170]

It would be a posthumous libel to claim Bülow's commitment to Brahms was merely an act of revenge directed at Wagner. For there was one thing Bülow had in common with Brahms: unconditional fidelity to the original text of a work, and it was this shared purism that brought the two musicians together. His rigorous musical self-discipline proved ideal for Brahms's music. His motto was, 'Emotion without thought is mawkishness.'[171] Early encounters between the two had not led to any collaboration, but even in 1854 the conductor had, as he wrote to his mother on 6 January 1854, seen in 'Schumann's young prophet . . . a very likeable, candid character with something divinely ordained – in the best sense of the word – about his talent'. Since 1880 Bülow had been building up and training a model orchestra in Meiningen, and Brahms began to visit. While others expressed surprise at the growing friendship between Bülow and Brahms, the latter insisted that his visits to Meiningen were quite natural:

The conductor and pianist Hans von Bülow (1830–94) studied with Liszt, before making his first tour in 1853. Later he married Liszt's daughter Cosima. She left him for Wagner after Bülow conducted the premiere of *Die Meistersinger* in 1868. He was the dedicatee of Tchaikovsky's First Piano Concerto. When he condemned Verdi's *Requiem*, Bülow's great friend Brahms wrote: *Bülow has given himself away ('hat sich blamiert'): Verdi's Requiem is a work of genius.*

. . . *you and others probably don't take a simple enough view of my 'Bülow-trips'.*

The main reason I was in Meiningen was to be able to play and rehearse a new piano concerto in peace and without the uncomfortable prospect of a concert. That's something I can't do anywhere else. This wouldn't have been thought strange if I'd gone elsewhere, even if I had selected the biggest ass of a musical director.

So why is it thought strange that I chose to come here with B? He is certainly a very idiosyncratic and very argumentative man, but

Hans von Bülow and Brahms

nevertheless intelligent, serious and competent. You must also realize how outstandingly his people have been trained; and so when someone like me comes along and makes music with them, they can do it straight from the heart. I really don't know where I could do any better.

I assure you that during the winter – if the music should chance to appear and people think they've worked ever so hard and achieved ever so much – I'll often think back with longing to those truly industrious players and their magnificent achievements.[172]

Bülow himself countered malicious remarks, such as a report in the *Berliner Tageblatt* that 'Brahms is about to go to Meiningen to study his own second piano concerto under Hans v. Bülow', with evident pleasure: 'In accordance with a promise he made to the undersigned, Herr Dr Brahms intends to do the court orchestra, of which the undersigned is the director, the honour of reviewing and, if necessary, correcting their studies of his symphonic works; at the same time he also intends to use the occasion of his visit, arranged for the 17th [of the month], to try out his new piano concerto for the first time with orchestral accompaniment. The studying will be all on our side.'[173]

The friendship with Bülow lasted a long time, but like other Brahms partnerships, it eventually broke down. Bülow was hurt when Brahms conducted his Fourth Symphony twice instead of just once in Frankfurt, for they had initially agreed that Bülow should conduct the second performance there. In point of fact the two had already begun to get on each other's nerves while on tour together, although they must also have had fun with the Second Piano Concerto, one playing while the other conducted at one performance, then swapping roles for the next.

Clara Schumann was surely right in her assessment when she wrote in her diary of January 1882, 'Everywhere he goes, Brahms enjoys triumphs of a kind hardly ever seen before for a composer. The performance of his works by the Meiningen orchestra is only partly responsible . . . Given his high position as a creative artist, I felt his tour with Bülow was beneath his dignity, but now that his full significance has been presented to the world, I am pleased and happy for him; however great the composer may be in himself, public recognition still raises him above himself . . .'[174]

The breach with Bülow was healed two years later, although, as with the rift with Joseph Joachim, the old warmth never returned. At least it was Brahms who took the first step, perhaps after all feeling some guilt over the affair. When Bülow arrived in Vienna on a leg of one of his concert tours, Brahms sent a visiting card to his hotel, on which he had simply written the notes of Pamina's '*Soll ich dich, Teurer, nicht mehr sehn?*' (Shall I see you no more, beloved?). Bülow, meanwhile, always remained a vigorous proponent of Brahms's music, making good his declared intention of 'winning over for him that part of the nation that was not interested in him'.[175] Just as he educated his orchestra,

Bülow regarded educating the public as one of his tasks. He often performed two works by Brahms on the same programme, and certainly contributed to the better understanding of certain major works.

Meiningen was not only significant in Brahms's history because of its connection with Bülow and his elite orchestra; it was also where Brahms found 'his' duke. Georg II and his wife, Baroness von Heldburg, were what one might call, almost without irony, 'artistically inclined'. Brahms liked visiting a court where the ruler would put up with him calling out to him after his early morning walk, *Ah, Your Highness, I've just had a little pre-breakfast stroll round the neighbouring principalities.*[176] The duke's regard for the composer resulted in his being made commander of the Meiningen order of knighthood, and later receiving an even higher decoration. Brahms's mixed reaction to these honours, a combination of casual gratitude and a degree of irritation, can be seen from the letters in which he attempted to deal with his elevation to a higher rank. The first, to the baroness, shows how easy and at home Brahms felt at this court, while illustrating his intense disdain for letter writing:

Dear and esteemed Baroness Heldberg,

I keep putting off sending you a few words of thanks. As long as I'm sitting staring at the blank sheet of paper I have the most delightful conversation with you. Writing intrudes on it – but that only tells you how much I enjoy thinking back, and how gratefully. Anyway, it's an affair of state on which I have to write to you. I do not have the relevant volume of the Almanach de Gotha *to hand, nor can I decipher the relevant signature, so do not know the name of the minister I should approach. That being the case, is it contrary to all* raison d'état *if I should take the liberty of sending back my knight commander's cross to you? As you know, I now have a new, even greater sign of His Majesty's grace and favour to wear. You should have seen it in all its glory in Leipzig, you should have seen the delight with which Director Stägemann checked my toilette!*[177]

He had also already written to his housekeeper in Vienna, Celestine Truxa, about the decoration:

I'd like to ask you to do me a favour, if it's not too much trouble. In the wardrobe where I keep my linen there's a cigar box with the decorations you've sewn together. Could you send it to me here in Meiningen? (Meiningen, The Castle, Duchy of Meiningen) – Next to it is a little case with a star in it. If you can put this in as well, with or without its case, then please do so, and I wouldn't mind a couple of pairs of socks as well. – If there's any problem at all packing these up and sending them off, then don't bother. It's not essential, not at all.[178]

His tendency to put comfort before honour peaked in his twice-repeated refusal to travel to England to receive an honorary doctorate from Cambridge. He talked about the *great honour*, but then went on, *Above all, I would ask you to be kind enough to bear in mind that I can't go to Cambridge without going to London as well, and in London I should be visiting and doing goodness knows how many things – all this in the beautiful summer weather when I am sure you would much rather be taking a stroll with me beside a beautiful Italian lake.*[179]

Brahms in 1883

This free-and-easy attitude famously translated to his outward appearance. Brahms just did not see why he should torture himself with a collar and so preferred to wear, concealed beneath the large beard he wore from the age of 50, a collarless Jaeger shirt. When the Austrians conferred the Order of St Leopold upon him, his Viennese friends joked, 'Now at least he'll have something to wear around his neck, though it's still not a collar.'[180]

Among these Viennese friends was one who, despite belonging to the cultured middle classes who often praised Brahms only to show off their own 'good taste' and to bask in his success, still managed to influence him. This was Theodor Billroth (1829–94) who, being intelligent, musical and musically trained, could offer Brahms more than just the hospitality of his house. He did in fact offer him hospitality as well, which Brahms enjoyed very much, although not so much as to express his gratitude by conforming to the social norm, and in this lay the seed of later discord. Billroth himself also committed a *faux pas* that Brahms simply could not comprehend. He cut out the first line from the manuscript of the A minor String Quartet Op 51, which Brahms had sent him, and framed it to hang on his wall. Though committed out of admiration and, it goes without saying, a certain ostentation, Brahms never forgave this act of cultural vandalism. Up to this point, the friendship had long provided great mutual pleasure. 'This morning,' Billroth wrote to his daughter on 19 November 1893, 'I enjoyed two very interesting hours with Brahms. He spoke very animatedly about the structure of melody and demonstrated to me the beauty of Bach's sarabandes. He can be so charming and friendly, one just regrets that he is not always like that.'[181]

The delight Brahms took in his discussions with the cultured doctor, as well as his continuing interest in theoretical questions, can be seen in the list he drew up as a result of a disagreement with Billroth about the relative statistical frequencies of major and minor keys. Using a precise list of works by Beethoven, Mozart, Haydn and Clementi, Brahms proved he was right. He sought to moderate the effect of his *Schadenfreude*, however, by giving the list the title: *Statistical Analysis of Major and Minor. Motto: (Prince Hal) Thus we play the fools with time, and the spirits of the wise sit in the clouds and mock us.*[182]

That Brahms had confidence in Billroth's sensitive yet critical understanding of music is clear from his letters: *Dearest friend,* he wrote in 1876, *I wish there were two words I could say this in, since several are insufficient to tell you properly how grateful I am for these last few days, which finished with your lunch yesterday.*

I wouldn't exactly say that my bit of composing is nothing but toil and trouble, just a constant annoyance that nothing better comes along – but you wouldn't believe how heart-warming sympathetic interest such as yours is; at such moments one thinks it is the best part of composing and everything to do with it. It is rare for one to come across someone who can display it as perfectly as you do . . .[183]

Theodor Billroth (1829–94) was a distinguished surgeon and a pioneer in early intestinal surgery. A highly trained amateur musician and virulent opponent of Wagner, he became a close friend of the critic Hanslick, who edited his *Wer ist Musikalisch?* (Who is musical?), two years after Billroth's death. He ran a series of musical soirées in Vienna, at which nearly all of Brahms's chamber music was played, with Billroth playing viola. Brahms dedicated his first two string quartets Op 51 to him.

Brahms also went on his first trip to Italy with Billroth. He was to go there nine times in all, sometimes with Billroth, sometimes with other friends, above all the Swiss writer Josef Viktor Widmann. Brahms was so relaxed on holiday in Italy and Sicily that his friends hardly recognized him. As so often happens with even the most self-absorbed individuals, he clearly felt liberated in a foreign and completely different environment. Elisabet von Herzogenberg, his friend back in far-off Leipzig, had felt it herself. In a letter to Brahms she eloquently described what he must have been feeling: 'Let me just congratulate you on having set foot in Italy. I am so glad I know Siena and can picture your delight when you come into that amphitheatre-like market place . . . Ah, how beautiful everything is there, how luxuriant, how natural and not artificial, such a delightful profusion of light and warmth and unconscious beauty that one ends up accepting it all as a matter of course.'[184]

All his other trips away from Vienna were either concert tours, or to spend the summer working in some beautiful spot. Nature was very important to him, as it had been to Beethoven. He loved walking in the countryside, both woods and mountains, and without a doubt, these were creative walks. Max Kalbeck writes: 'Later on in Ischl I had the unexpected opportunity of observing Brahms at work. An early riser and nature-lover like him, I had gone out very early one warm July morning. Suddenly I saw, hurrying across the meadow towards me, a man whom I first took for a farmer. Afraid that I was trespassing, I was already preparing myself for all kinds of unpleasantness when, to my delight, my angry farmer turned out to be none other than Brahms. But what a state he was in! And his dress! Bare-headed and in shirt sleeves, with no waistcoat or collar, he was waving his hat in one hand while dragging his jacket behind him in the grass with the other, and rushing along so quickly you would have thought there was an invisible pursuer at his heels. Even from a distance I could hear him wheezing and groaning. His hair was hanging over his face, and as he came nearer I could see the sweat pouring down his flushed cheeks. His eyes were fixed in front of him, staring into space, gleaming like those of some beast of prey – he gave the impression of being a man possessed. Before I had recovered from the shock, he had shot past me, so close we almost brushed against each other.'[185]

Whether it was Bad Ischl, Lichtenthal near Baden-Baden, Tutzing on the Starnberger See, or the Baltic island of Rügen, whether it was three summers on Lake Thun, a further three in Pörtschach on Wörther See or two in Mürzzuschlag in Styria, all Brahms's vacations were working summers. In the long run, when he became more set in his ways, Bad Ischl became his favourite summer residence.

Particular friends were associated with the different summer destinations. In Baden-Baden he was introduced by Julius

Allgeyer, a young copper engraver and close friend, to the painter Anselm Feuerbach (1829–80). There were the beginnings of a friendship between them, which may have come from agreement in their views on art, though it is difficult today to see the parallels between Feuerbach's allegorical painting and Brahms's 'absolute' music. After he was appointed professor at the Vienna Academy in 1873, Feuerbach started a portrait of Brahms, but when the latter advised him not to exhibit his *Battle of the Amazons* in Vienna, Feuerbach is said to have taken the portrait down from his easel and never touched it again.

Ischl meant Johann Strauss. 'Brahms was quite straightforwardly fond of his music. He had already enjoyed Strauss concerts in Baden-Baden. When Strauss wrote the first bars of *The Blue Danube* on his stepdaughter's fan, Brahms added, and presumably not merely as a joke, *Unfortunately not by Johannes Brahms*.'[186]

Not by Johannes Brahms is something that could also be written over every opera ever composed. For even though Brahms toyed with the notion of writing an opera for many years, he never did so. He wasn't afraid of Wagner, but may perhaps have been intimidated by his output. Whether or not it was the long shadow of Wagner that prevented him producing an opera, he himself always blamed the subject matter on offer. He said that he had simply never found one that appealed to him. Perhaps it was lucky that he did not torture himself with the

Brahms and Johann Strauss, whom he greatly admired. Strauss even invited him to contribute an episode to one of his waltzes, which Brahms was delighted to do.

attempt; his much admired Franz Schubert made repeated, and it has to be said, unsuccessful attempts on the form, and the endeavour was largely a vale of tears.

Among the many opera subjects offered to Brahms, or which he drew to the attention of potential librettists, two were discussed over a long period. Both were based on plays by the Venetian writer Carlo Gozzi (1720–1806); the one Brahms preferred, *König Hirsch (King Stag)*, even made it to the opera stage in 1956, as the first popularly successful stage work by *the* great German opera composer of the 20th century, Hans Werner Henze. Julius Allgeyer proposed another suggestion based on a Gozzi text, *Das Laute Geheimnis (The Loud Secret)*. Indeed Gozzi's writing seemed a good choice as the basis for the kind of opera Brahms had in mind to write, namely the kind of opera that would be a pleasant contrast to Wagner's 'heavy' operas. Brahms also tried to get Paul Heyse, a multi-talented and fluent writer, to produce a libretto. But nothing ever came of these plans. After his initial enthusiasm, Brahms hesitated, ignoring Allgeyer's sketches and the many suggestions of his 'agent' in Italy, the experienced librettist Josef Viktor Widmann. The cause of his hesitation was perhaps the incompleteness of the sketches, but certainly also due to his musical idealism. Problematically, what he wished to write was not an opera, but the 'essence' of an opera. The prospect of writing music for parts of a plot that did not 'need' music was anathema to him.

It was not a question of Brahms's not being able to master the drama; that he had mastered it was demonstrated clearly enough in his music. It was rather that he was afraid his music would be trivialized. In line with current fashion and with an eye on Wagner, Brahms was attracted by the idea of having his say in this area of music as well as in others. But by this time, opera was perhaps above all a genre for young composers who were trying to attract attention; and at the point when Brahms was considering writing an opera, he was far from being in need of a kick-start to his career. In the end the urge to write an opera revealed itself to be little more than a diversion. Music theatre was not for him, and he knew it. Not only that, but he actually did not much like the opera of his time, not even Wagner's operas, despite all that was said about him being 'the best Wagnerian'. He was, however, drawn to the theatre and often attended performances at the Burgtheater in Vienna, but was hardly attracted to the Opera at all. After a while he simply said it was too late for him to start writing an opera, in the same way as it was now too late for him to risk getting married. At some point or other he was simultaneously attracted to and repulsed by both things, but ultimately they were ideas he merely flirted with.

Nevertheless, his reaction to the announcement of the forthcoming marriage of Julie Schumann to an Italian count in 1869, when he was 36 years old, was one of surprise and consternation. For Brahms had seen her as his bride-to-be, without, however, ever saying anything to her. Once again it was the world at large that reaped the benefit; after hearing the news, he composed

The autograph of the *Alto Rhapsody* Op 53

the *Alto Rhapsody* Op 53, referring to it as his 'bridal song'. Clara Schumann understood this background when she wrote in her diary, 'I cannot but see the piece as the expression of his own heartfelt anguish; if only he could speak like that in words.'[187]

When Brahms was about 50 he was once again smitten with

a feeling that took him for a time beyond mere flirtation with the idea of marriage. The object of his affection was a young contralto, Hermine Spies, who, despite the 24 year age difference between them, perhaps expected the celebrated composer who was so charming to her to propose. But it never happened; the only

German contralto Hermine Spies, who hoped Brahms would propose to her

outcome of this affair was the composition of two collections of songs, Op 96 and 97. These included *Wir wandelten, wir zwei zusammen* (We wander, we two together) and *Komm bald* (Come soon). 'What a lovely surprise the new songs you sent me were,' wrote Theodor Billroth. 'If they really are new, then the fires must be burning as fiercely as ever, which is not surprising, given your robust health. I have the feeling there's something behind them. To put it another way: one doesn't choose that kind of poem and write that kind of song just to produce another composition. How splendid for you! And for us!'[188]

A few years before this episode, another old desire had also resurfaced: Brahms's never abandoned hope of having a permanent position. Although by this time it would not have made economic sense for him to take up such a position, between October 1876 and February 1877 he entered into serious negotiations with the city of Düsseldorf. Brahms, who *hated nothing so much as writing paper, especially when it was waiting for important business matters to be recorded on it*,[189] found himself drafting letters to the president of the Düsseldorf Music Society setting out his conditions. All of these came down to the often repeated word 'independence'; and he even put forward another candidate right from the start. He could not, he wrote, *suppress the question: how is it that the name of Max Bruch didn't immediately occur to you?*[190] Brahms eventually broke off these negotiations, which probably came as no surprise to Düsseldorf; his attitude to permanent positions was already well known there. A leaflet on the state of music in Düsseldorf, entitled 'An appeal to the sense of justice of our citizens and their representatives' contains some pertinent remarks on the negotiations with Brahms. 'Johannes Brahms knows Düsseldorf, he stayed here in Schumann's time, and we know him as an ingenious composer. We know him as a conductor, too, in that he conducted his *Schicksalslied {Song of Fate}* Op 54 at the last music festival; and we also know that he has never kept a position for any length of time, because artistic freedom is necessary for his compositions. Given this situation, it is not unlikely that Brahms . . . should he accept the position in spite of everything . . . would only keep it for one or two years at most.'[191] No one, looking back with the advantage of hindsight, would want to contradict this statement.

He was also offered Bach's old post of 'Cantor' the Thomaskirche in Leipzig and turned it down right away; when, three years before his death, he was finally offered the direction of the Philharmonic concerts in Hamburg, his answer was inevitable:

There are few things I desired for so long and so fervently at one time – but that means at the right time! – And it took a long time for me

Max Bruch (1838–1920) was best known during his lifetime as a composer of large choral works such as the cantata *Odysseus*; today, however, he is remembered for his violin concerti and *Kol Nidrei* for cello and orchestra. He was the Kapellmeister of the Prince of Schwarzenburg-Sonderhausen from 1827–70, and from 1880–83 the conductor and musical director of the Liverpool Philharmonic Orchestra.

The organist and symphonist Anton Bruckner (1824–96) might best be described as the composer who expressed the Wagnerian aesthetic symphonically; ironically, the medium that Wagner had famously declared dead. His relationship with Brahms was complicated by this adulation, and the two never managed to repair their differences, even though they were both closely involved with the Conservatoire in Vienna. Bruckner also suffered the opprobrium of the critic Hanslick, and somewhat pathetically, upon receiving a decoration from the Emperor Franz Joseph, implored him to silence his critic.

to become accustomed to the fact that I had to look elsewhere. – If things had gone according to my wishes, I might today be celebrating my 30th anniversary with you. You, however, would be in the same situation as you are today, namely of having to look for a capable younger director. I hope you find him, and I hope he devotes himself to the business with as much good will, reasonable ability and as wholeheartedly as would have your most respectful and devoted J Brahms.[192] By the time that Brahms wrote these words he had long since won the battle for recognition; after Wagner's death he was almost unanimously acclaimed as 'the first', even if Anton Bruckner had been set up as a kind of 'anti-pope'.

In the last years of his life Brahms no longer needed to struggle. His oeuvre was as good as complete. One could say, without disparagement, that the solid bourgeois citizen had taken over from the unattached artist. It is even almost comforting to see a man's life slowly coming to its natural end, an end that corresponded to the inner nature of one who had always forced himself to allow his compositions time, and who always viewed these works with a cold critical eye that did not desert him, even in old age. *As a farewell to Ischl, I threw a lot of torn-up manuscript paper into the* [river] *Traun*,[193] he wrote in 1890.

Brahms's last great work, which, out of fear of his own feelings, he called *Schnadahüpfeln* after a type of popular song that often ended with a yodel, was the *Four Serious Songs* Op 121. His refusal to admit openly how deeply this piece of music affected him is revealed by the letter to his publisher in which he says that he would like to dedicate these *little songs* to Max Klinger. Klinger was an artist who had sent Brahms 41 engravings of a 'Brahms Fantasy' as a New Year present for 1894, and whose father had just died. *This will show you that they are not exactly a joke – on the contrary, they are damn' serious and at the same time so profane the police might prohibit them, were it not that the words are all to be found in the Bible.*[194]

Brahms, who was bound by tradition, also stood, much more than his contemporaries, who believed themselves to be living in an 'enlightened' secular age, in the Christian tradition. But he revealed so little of himself, it is almost impossible to say whether or not he saw it as more than just a tradition. However, death was certainly a subject that occupied his thoughts throughout his life. He 'sang' of it so often in his *Lieder* that it almost makes one feel he was on familiar terms with it. On the other hand, his trepidation before his own *Four Serious Songs,* which he refused to listen to in the concert hall, suggests a fear of death and a certain reluctance to scry further into the unknown. None of this can be seen in the robust and rather self-sufficient figure 'on his way to the Red Hedgehog',[195] but the 'dying fall' of his melodies that characterizes almost the whole of his output gives us a glimpse of his real sorrow at the transience of human life.

Clara Schumann died on 20 May 1896. Brahms was delayed on the way to her funeral, but met the cortege en route to the graveyard. On this journey he was infected with the fever that

Brahms and the Red Hedgehog

eventually led to his own illness.[196] His next pieces were composed reeling from the shock of the death of this lifelong friend, and in one of them he went back, musically, to the past, right back to the beginning in which this end was prefigured. While Robert Schumann was dying in the clinic in Endenich, Brahms and Clara had spent much time studying sacred music and he had written down the tunes of several chorales. This was now 40 years ago, but actually Brahms was looking back even farther. As a boy in Hamburg, while attending Pastor Petersen's classes on Christian doctrine, it was the chorales that had made the deepest impression on him. Now, at the 'last hour', they resurfaced from the depths of his memory.

In this work, the 11 Choral Preludes, Op 122, Brahms once again, and for the very last time, combined standard musical material and individual treatment. He perhaps had the 'Cantor of the Thomaskirche', Bach, in mind. In a personal profession of faith, Bach had changed the opening line of the chorale on which his own last organ prelude was based from *Wenn wir in höchsten Nöten sein* (When in the hour of utmost need) to *Vor Deinem Thron tret ich hiermit* (Before Thy throne, my God, I stand). Brahms's last music was written – and it was no mere accident – to the tune of the chorale *O Welt ich mss dich lassen* (Oh world I must now leave you). It was suffused with pain. On the empty stave after the last notes of this chorale prelude is the date: *June 96. Ischl.*

Brahms was already ill by the time he returned to Ischl from

Clara's funeral in Düsseldorf, and the 'common-or-garden jaundice,'[197] as his doctor called it, from which he suffered, was to cause his death. Cancer of the liver was the first real diagnosis, but this was kept secret from Brahms. It was often also quoted later as the cause of his death, but he actually died from pancreatic carcinoma, which was for a long time known in Viennese medical jargon as 'morbus Brahms' (Brahms disease).

Brahms went to Carlsbad and returned to Vienna feeling worse than ever. He drafted a will with his friend Dr Fellinger, in whose house he had been a frequent guest (and whose wife, Maria Fellinger, took the best photographs of Brahms in old age),

Brahms, 6 October 1895. One of the remarkable pictures taken by Maria Fellinger

however, he never formalized it, for fear of being forced to admit to himself that his illness was terminal. As a result, his testament was the subject of a lawsuit that lasted for years.

Brahm's public not only followed his coffin in their thousands on his death, but also demonstrated their affection for him in the concert hall, when he made his last appearance at the Musikverein at a concert given by the Vienna Philharmonic. 'Hans Richter conducted the Fourth Symphony and made up for the first careless and uncaring performance with a monumental and perfect reading of the work. The public was in a frenzy of enthusiasm. But when Richter pointed to the box, bringing to their attention for the first time that the composer himself was sitting there, deathly pale, a hurricane of applause

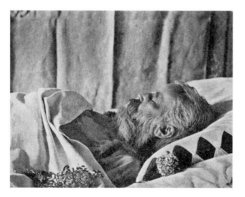
Brahms on his deathbed

broke out, which grew after each movement. The calls, cries and clapping were deafening, people stood on their seats to have a better view of the master's terribly ravaged figure, and waved their hats and handkerchiefs at him, and he was obliged to come to the front of the box again and again, and at the close the thunder of acclamation was never-ending. The audience knew they were seeing Brahms for the last time, and he knew it as well.'[198]

In his final illness Brahms still took an active interest in what was going on, and gave vigorous support, for example, to the appointment of Gustav Mahler as director of the Vienna Opera, for he had found his *Don Giovanni* unforgettable. During these last days and hours, his friends tried to comfort the composer, who would have preferred to ignore his illness, by giving him hope, even though they knew there was none. On 3 April 1897, at around nine in the morning Johannes Brahms died, in his apartment at 4 Karlsgasse, Vienna.

The dispute over music: Liszt, Wagner and Bruckner

Over the years, a group, or school, had formed around Franz Liszt, taking his phrase – 'music of the future' as its rallying cry. Its headquarters were in Weimar, where Liszt had 'held court' since 1848, and its mouthpiece was the *Neue Zeitschrift für Musik*, originally founded by Schumann and now edited by Franz Brendel. Max Kalbeck calls Brendel 'the generalissimo of the new German music',[199] for the 'musicians of the future' were generally known as the 'New Germans'. Liszt and his followers demanded that music should have a programme, and this provides the third, and clearest, designation for the Liszt school: 'programme musicians'. The musical vehicle for this

Franz Liszt by B Plockhorst, 1857

approach was the 'tone poem'; and Liszt wrote 12 of them. In a later assessment of Liszt, Brahms said, *The child prodigy, the travelling virtuoso and the socialite ruined the composer before he had even got properly started.*[200]

That it was Robert Schumann who promoted Brahms, in, for example, his article 'New Paths', was bound to arouse a sceptical response from the New Germans, since Schumann had very definitely distanced himself from them. He had offended both Liszt and Wagner, whom the New German School proclaimed their standard bearers. He had, for example, returned the score of *The*

Flying Dutchman to Wagner with the comment that it was too 'Meyerbeer-y' for him. It was perhaps a combination of his attachment to Schumann and his lack of a clear understanding of his own standpoint that fuelled the 27-year-old Brahms's pugnacity: *My fingers often itch to start a fight, to write some anti-Liszts. Me! Who can't even write to his dearest friend for lack of material.*[201]

However, in 1860, Brahms, Joseph Joachim, Julius Otto Grimm and Bernhard Scholz did launch a campaign against the New Germans, but without much success. Indeed it came across as clumsy, stilted and over-personalized, and the opposition had great fun pulling it to pieces. 'The Declaration', which was published prematurely and only carried the names of the four originators, expressed regret at the *Neue Zeitschrift*'s claim that 'all serious musicians were in fundamental agreement with the movement it represented.' In fact, they pointed out, they, the undersigned 'do not recognize the principles laid down by Brendel's journal and can only lament and condemn the products of the leaders and pupils of the so-called "New German School", which are partly a practical application of those principles and partly demand the elaboration of more and more new, unheard-of theories that are contrary to the innermost being of music'.[207]

The answer to this rather high-flown declaration was a parody of it:

'Public Protest:

We, the undersigned, also want to play first violin and therefore protest against everything that places obstacles in the way of our rise to that position – namely against the increasing influence of the movement in music designated the "New German School" by Dr Brendel as, indeed, against all manifestations of the spirit in music. After these things they find so unpleasant have been destroyed, they propose to set up immediately for all like-minded colleagues a "League for unexciting and boring music".

The editors of *Music of the Futile*

(Signed) J Fiddler, Hans Newpath, H Henpecked, Riff Raff, Tom, Dick and Harry.'[208]

'J Fiddler' was Joachim, and 'Hans Newpath', in an allusion to Schumann's article in praise of him, was of course Brahms.

There have always been as many cliques in music as in every sphere of human activity. Brahms, however, was the last person capable of heading a party or an opposition group; a loner from choice, he was unsuited to the role of leader. Even the contrast with Wagner could not rouse him to action; the battle cry of 'Wagner or Brahms' came from others. There was virtually no personal contact at all between the two composers. Their one meeting produced nothing of any great significance apart from a moderately positive quotation by Wagner about Brahms: 'You can see what the old forms are still capable of,' he said after Brahms had played his *Handel Variations* Op 24, 'when someone comes along who knows how to treat them.'[204]

Wagner 'not a man to mince words'

In general, however, Wagner was not a man to mince words. In his essay 'On Conducting', which appeared in 1869, he pronounced judgment on all those who were not in Liszt's camp and spoke contemptuously of 'St Johannes', of 'musical mediocrity' and 'mealy-mouthed bigotry', of which he himself had formerly been accused.[205]

Brahms held back. 'He never made disparaging remarks about

Wagner,' wrote Klaus Groth in his memoir of Brahms, 'Once, when we saw derogatory criticism of Wagner in a newspaper, Brahms said to me, *And I am presumed to be the real source of all such comments, I who know Wagner better than any of them!*'[206]

There is some surviving correspondence between Brahms and Wagner that tells us something about their different temperaments and also something about their assessment of each other. They write to one another in lofty tones, like two sovereigns, whose courtly environment forbids more familiar exchanges, although Brahms does occasionally break out of the stiff formality. The subject of the correspondence was a Wagner manuscript, a revision to a scene from *Tannhäuser*, which had been given as a present to Brahms by his friend Tausig. Wagner took the view that he had given the manuscript to Tausig to look after. 'Presumably it is quite unnecessary,' Wagner wrote, 'for me to remind you of these circumstances, and no further discussion will be needed to induce you to be so good and kind as to return this manuscript, which you can only value as a curiosity, while my son might treasure it as a memento.'[207]

Brahms returned the manuscript:

While stating right away that I will 'be so good and kind' as to return the manuscript in question, I must nevertheless permit myself to add a few words . . .

Given the large number of your works, ownership of this scene can hardly be as valuable to your son as to me, who, without actually being a collector, nevertheless likes to have autographs that I treasure. 'Curiosities' I do not collect . . . And now Brahms abandons some of his reserve: *I almost believe I owe it to myself to reply in greater detail to your letter . . . but I fear it would be impossible to avoid being misunderstood for, if you will permit me, the saying about eating cherries* [referring to the German expression 'It is not a good idea to eat cherries with great men', in other words, don't tangle with the powerful] *could hardly be more appropriate than for someone like* me *vis-à-vis* you. But perhaps you might prefer it if I could no longer regard myself as having made you a present. Should that be the case, I will say that, since you are robbing my autograph collection of a treasure, it would please me greatly if my library were to be enriched by one more of your works, perhaps the Meistersinger.'[208]

Instead of a score of the *Meistersinger*, which he was 'completely out of', Wagner sent a score of *Rheingold*, writing, 'Occasionally the charge has been made that my musical things are stage sets; *Rheingold* will suffer greatly from that criticism. On the other hand, it might perhaps be not uninteresting to observe, in following the scores of the subsequent parts of *The Ring of the Nibelungen**, how I have managed to derive all kinds of thematic material from the scenery I set up here. Looked at in this light, perhaps of all my works *Rheingold* might find a sympathetic judge in you.

> With most respectful greetings
>> from your very devoted and indebted
>>> Richard Wagner.'[209]

Brahms's answer shows serious and in-depth study of Wagner's music, whilst not admiring it:

Indeed, the best, the right kind of thanks is directed daily at the work itself – it is not lying around unused. Maybe this part does not initially stimulate one to the kind of detailed study your great work as a whole demands; but this Rheingold *has passed through your very own hands, however brightly the* Valkyrie's *beauty may shine, putting the chance advantage of precedence in the shade. But pardon this sort of comment. The more likely cause is that we do scant justice to a part that makes us want to look beyond it to the whole. With this work we are happy to content ourselves with the part for some considerable time.*

For do we not have the inspiring, though strange delight – like Romans unearthing a gigantic statue – of watching the whole work emerge and come to life bit by bit. The only compensation for the thankless task you have of observing our astonishment and criticism is the certainty you feel within you and the ever more widespread and growing acclaim your magnificent works enjoy.[210]

There were several occasions on which Brahms was on the point of going to Bayreuth, but he always drew back out of fear of the sensation it would cause. *The fact that I just can't make up my mind about going to Bayreuth must be a sign that the 'Yes' doesn't want to come out. I hardly need say that I'm afraid of the Wagnerians and that they could spoil my pleasure at the best of Wagner.*[211] He also found it difficult to accept that a good friend, such as the conductor Hermann Levi, should champion Wagner's music as much as his.

The least one can say about Brahms's attitude to other composers of his time is that it was far from consistent, and verging on the contradictory. Meanwhile, he was fairly modest about his own music, particularly when comparing it with that of earlier composers, even if at times he was not unhappy with his achievements: *Yes, I'm not ashamed to say that it gives me great pleasure whenever I feel that a song, an andante or anything else has turned out well. And just imagine how the gods – Mozart, Beethoven and those who produce such things day in day out – must have felt when they wrote 'finis' under* The Marriage of Figaro *and* Fidelio, *then got down to* Don Giovanni, *and the Ninth Symphony the very next day. I just cannot understand how people like us can feel vain.*[212]

He was irritated by what he felt was excessive praise. Clara Schumann was forced to defend herself: 'How I enjoyed your folk songs, my dear Johannes – if only I was allowed to talk about them the way my heart feels! But I sense more and more that I must learn to hold myself in check. It hurts me terribly to have to do so towards you in musical matters, for you should and must know that it is not blind enthusiasm for you speaking . . . You don't see or hear me speaking about you to others, dear Johannes; I really do not get overexcited. But that I am often powerfully moved by the wealth of your genius, that you always seem to me to be one on whom Heaven has showered its fairest gifts and that I love and admire you for so many magnificent qualities – all this is true, dearest Johannes, and has taken deep root in my heart, so do not try to kill it all within me by your cold philosophizing – it is impossible.'[213]

Brahms's attitude to the music of his contemporaries was pretty defensive; there are, perhaps, two reasons for this. On the one hand, as he became more and more famous and admired, ever more compositions by second- and third-rate composers were sent to him, which he was unwilling either to reject out of hand, especially if they came from close friends, or to praise against his own conviction. He took this task seriously, but developed an all-purpose style of gruff benevolence for his answers, which, of course, came naturally to him. He even adopted it when he was not dealing with second-rate composers. His *Very nice* [214] to Richard Strauss, for example, even though accompanied by a few pieces of practical advice, is not really much better than the *Tell me, where do you procure this lovely manuscript paper?*,[215] which was Max Bruch's reward for showing him a big oratorio. Strauss, incidentally, took his revenge by coining the name 'Lederner Johannes' ('Johannes Dryasdust').

The second reason for his resistance to contemporary developments in music was a perceptible concern that he might see the place he had won in the hierarchy of modern music placed under threat. His driving ambition had resulted in an almost insatiable hunger for external recognition and the desire to be regarded as 'the first'. He could accept composers who were already established and take a relatively sanguine view of them, as his attitude to Wagner shows. But he rejected contemporary trends or ideas that appeared after he had already finalized his concept of music, sure that these new paths, which were leading to a dissolution of tonality, could not be his. As he got older, he even began to reject things without looking at them first. However, he did recognize Gustav Mahler's First Symphony, at least its Scherzo, as the work of a genius, but added a disparaging rider to his assessment: *Until now I was under the impression that Richard Strauss was the leader of the revolution, but I now see that Mahler is king of the subversives.*[216]

The complete lack of any understanding between Brahms and the composer Anton Bruckner has its origins in the early days of his antagonism with Liszt and the subsequent mutual provocation by the supporters of both sides. But the bitterness of his resentment towards Bruckner was unique: *Bruckner? That's something completely different* [from Gustav Mahler, and Hugo Wolf, whom he refused to judge because, he said, he lacked the necessary feeling or understanding]. *The important thing there, at least in the first instance, is not his compositions, but a con trick, which will be dead and forgotten in a year or two. You can make what you like of this: Bruckner owes his fame solely to me, and but for me nobody would have cared two hoots about him, though it happened very much against my will. Nietzsche once declared that I had become famous merely by chance, because the anti-Wagner party needed me as an anti-pope. That is nonsense, of course; I'm not the kind of man who would make a good leader for any party. I must go my way alone and in peace and I never crossed the path of others. But that was what happened with Bruckner. That is, after Wagner's death his party naturally needed a new 'pope', and the best they could do was Bruckner. Do you really believe that anyone in that immature crowd has the least notion of what these symphonic boa constrictors are about? And don't you think that I am the musician who knows and understands Wagner's works best today, at least better than any of his so-called followers, who would like nothing better than to poison me? I once told Wagner himself that I was the best Wagnerian around. Do you think I am too narrow-minded to be enchanted by the joy and greatness of* Meistersinger*? Or dishonest enough to conceal my view that I consider a few bars of this work to be worth more than all the operas that have been written since? Me an anti-pope? It's*

*too silly! And Bruckner's works immortal, or even symphonies? It's
ludicrous!*[217]

Could Brahms really not see Bruckner's genius? Maybe, he
simply kept his ears and eyes closed tight so as not to notice it,
or perhaps he saw Bruckner's music as part of the disintegration
of the musical canon, which for him was the equivalent of the
decline of western culture itself. The conductor and composer
Bernhard Paumgartner, who as a child had known Brahms, told
a strangely reassuring story. 'When Bruckner died in 1896 the
funeral service was held in the Karlskirche in Vienna. The whole
of Vienna poured in to attend the ceremony. This was my home
territory and, being familiar with every nook and cranny, I slipped
into the church by a side door and through the sacristy. To my
astonishment whom should I see, standing almost in the dark
and hidden from the public gaze by a pillar, but Johannes Brahms.
The tears were streaming down his gaunt cheeks, already marked
by the approach of death, and into his beard.'[218]

If Bruckner was *beyond music* for Brahms, there was one composer whose great talent he did recognize and to whom he gave
his wholehearted support. This musician was not an innovator,
and the two composers found common ground in their mutual
love of folk music. It was Antonín Dvořák (1841–1904), for
whom Brahms arranged a scholarship and whom he strongly recommended to his publisher. He was even content to proofread
for Dvořák, and he could openly admit, *I go green with envy when
I see the things that just come to him without effort.*[219] Of Dvořák he
could say, . . . *you are unlikely to find a more beautiful, more refreshing
impression of genuine, rich and attractive creative talent.*[220] Brahms
regarded Dvořák as his protégé, among his friends even. *If Dvořák
should happen to come to tomorrow's concert*, he wrote to the Austrian
industrial magnate, Victor von Miller zu Aichholz, in whose house
he took lunch every Sunday for a time, *and if he should be free,
would you have any objection if I should give him the pleasure of bringing*

Anton Dvořák by A Mitterfellner

In 1897, Brahms persuaded the cellist of the Joachim Quartet, Robert Hausmann, to come to his rooms and play through the Czech Antonín Dvořák's (1841–1904) cello concerto with him at the piano. Afterwards, he exclaimed: *Had I known that such a 'cello concerto as that could have been written, I would have tried to compose one myself.* Dvořák had earlier dedicated his D minor Quartet Op 34 to Brahms in 1877, in gratitude for the support that Brahms had given him, and which he continued to give for the rest of his life, consistently promoting the performance and publication of Dvořák's music.

him with me? He can eat from my plate and drink from my cup, and he doesn't (as far as I know) make speeches![221] He even offered Dvořák, who politely refused, as much money as he wanted from his private assets. It is almost as if the idea of having a younger contemporary, his equal in talent, to whom he could be benevolent, was liberating for Brahms.

On the other hand he regarded talents, such as Hugo Wolf in particular, as bitter opponents without any justification at all. *There wasn't much*, he said after a visit from the young Hugo Wolf, *to the compositions he brought along. I went through everything very closely with him and pointed out a few things. There's some talent there, but he takes things too lightly. I told him quite seriously what he lacked . . . At that he'd had enough and didn't come back. Now he's venting his spleen at me.*[222] Indeed, Hugo Wolf's reviews of Brahms's music represent a late blossoming of the dispute about music that had long since degenerated into a quarrel between cliques. For instance, he famously claimed that one single clash of the cymbals in Liszt expressed more feeling and intellect than all of Brahms's symphonies and serenades put together.[223] Today it is unnecessary to refute such a glaring error of judgment; there were contemporary assessments, much earlier than Wolf's reviews, which provided refutation in advance. One example is the following extract from a review of the First Piano Concerto in D minor, Op 15:

'And you heard nothing of that, you of the quick tongue and clumsy critical pen? – For you it's all just a barren waste and *infusoria* and unfermented dough? – What point would there be in explaining to you the profound and stately calm with which the Andante enters, immersing us, as it were, in the depths of our soul, there to seek peace from the turmoil of the world? Or the bubbling vigour with which the soul tears itself free from this rapt contemplation in the last movement to reconcile the two, the excitement of passion and the serenity of withdrawal from the world? The beauty and musicality of the way it plays with the material, the theme of the finale now full, now condensed, now dancing along, now grave, now as a fugue, now in free development? What point would there be in showing how the instrumentation is not only sumptuous and varied and always drawn in with a firm hand, but also has the most beautifully rich, often full organ sound? You would not understand, for you heard none of this.'[224]

Brahms's music

That great art is beyond classification is as true of music as it is of painting, sculpture and literature. Goethe, for many the epitome of German Classicism, was seen by the Romantics as the creator of the archetypal Romantic work in his novel *Wilhelm Meister Lehrjahre*. While Brahms, often regarded as the last representative of Classicism, is, on closer study, situated both between musical tradition and Romanticism on the one hand, and between Romanticism and incipient Modernism on the other. By extending the expressive range of existing forms, this great traditionalist took music into new if not – given that his starting point was traditional forms – entirely uncharted waters. In music, even less than in the other arts, there are no firm boundaries between epochs and certainly no points of culmination. Brahms realized this even as a young man when he came across the straitjacket into which the Austrian musicologist Karl Debrois van Bruyck (1828–1902) tried to force the history of music:

The most blinkered part of it is that this little fellow Debrois absolutely insists he can see the topmost pinnacle of the completed cathedral of music.

Who can ever say that something that never comes to an end has reached its end? Little men have always wanted to put a full stop after every genius. After Mozart, to stick with the last but one.[225]

He wrote this when he was 24. The acuity of the observation is not lessened by the fact that in old age, and by the time he himself was the composer in question, Brahms's opinion was quite different. He disapproved of the direction contemporary music was taking and had turned his back on it. He clearly liked repeating that he was the last person who still possessed a distinct sense of the integrity of music. In the course of a walk they took together in Ischl, he made this explicit to the young Gustav Mahler. They were going along the River Traun when 'Mahler suddenly took his arm and pointed down at the water with his other hand, exclaiming, "Look, Dr Brahms, look!" – *What is it?* Brahms asked. "Don't you see, there goes the last wave!" at which Brahms growled, *That's all very well, but perhaps what matters most is whether the wave flows out into the sea or ends up in a swamp.'*[226]

Those who are unwilling to see Brahms as the heir to Beethoven, and yet still want to place his music within a tradition, see Mendelssohn, Schumann and Brahms as a 'Central German Romantic School'.[227] Such constructs are doubtless not without their reasons and not without a certain justification, but they still do not match up to reality.

Of course, Brahms was part of a tradition, a continuity. Even Wagner, certainly the most independent-minded composer of the 19th century, who was repeatedly, perhaps not unjustly, accused of being an amateur of genius, only gradually freed himself from earlier models. But that proves that there were models. How much closer Brahms remained to the traditional hardly needs stating. Nevertheless, he was neither 'the heir to Beethoven', nor the final link in an imagined chain from Mendelssohn via Schumann; rather he placed himself quite consciously within the whole tradition of European music. Bach and Handel were composers he looked back to, but he equally revered Palestrina and Orlando di Lasso. He also used both medieval ecclesiastical modes and Flemish canonic techniques. In his vocal pieces, above all in his choral music, he wrote new music based on medieval, Renaissance and baroque forms. Throughout his life he never ceased to be amazed at the art of Johann Sebastian Bach:

Polyphony means with many voices, and nowadays one must distinguish carefully between having many voices and mere richness of sound.

Such a sea of notes from Bach can hardly be compared with others, can it?[228]

That he also looked back to Beethoven was so obvious that his only answer, when it was pointed out, was mockery. This is demonstrated in the famous anecdote about the aristocrat who, proud of his understanding of music, said to Brahms after a rehearsal of his C minor Symphony, 'It's remarkable how similar the C major theme in your finale is to the 'Joy' theme in the Ninth. *Yes*, he replied, *and even more remarkable is the fact that any ass can see it right away.*[229]

These references to and quotations of earlier music are a sign of a commitment to the past that Brahms took upon himself for all to see. Robert Schumann was the first to draw this starting point to the attention of the young Brahms in practical terms: 'Well – where is Johannes? Is he with you?' he wrote to Joachim. 'Give him my best wishes. Is he soaring – or just fluttering around among the flowers? Still no sound of trumpet, beat of drums? Tell him he should remember the openings of Beethoven's symphonies; he should try to do something similar.'[230]

Despite the musical echoes of Beethoven in his First Symphony in C minor, Brahms was not doing 'something similar'. The whole tension in his music comes from the way that the traditional forms he consciously adopts are transformed by a creative act to produce something entirely new and independent. This process is far from an effortless magic, but hard, concentrated work. This is discussed in a letter to Hans von Bülow:

I really do tend to envy my prolific colleagues the facility and speed with which they get things done. I'm quite prepared to assume they are not writing just to get into the encyclopaedia, but out of the same need, for the same reasons as I do – {to achieve} the best, that is. How often will someone like that cheerfully write his 'fine', which actually says, I'm finished with what I had in mind. While I can sometimes carry the smallest finished trifle about with me for a long time before reluctantly admitting it really is 'finished'![231]

His attitude to his own work corresponds to what the painter

Anselm Feuerbach claimed for himself: 'I was horrified at my initial lack of form; through tireless working at my compositions, coupled with the strictest observation, I have brought myself to the point where I can spot the tiniest faults at a glance.'[232] The will to succeed, which we have noted as characteristic of the 19th century, leads both artists to speak of the ideas that occur to them with something close to contempt: *What is actually called invention, that is a real idea, an inspiration, comes from above, so to speak, which means I can do nothing about it. From the moment it arrives, my contempt for this 'gift' is unbounded; I have to work without ceasing to make it my very own, well-earned, legal property. And that doesn't happen overnight.*[233]

Brahms seldom talked about his work or compositions. *I speak through my music,*[234] he wrote to Clara Schumann, and again and again, *I would love to write to you just in music.*[235] There is one subject connected with his work, however, that Brahms did talk about at some length, and not without reason, and this was variation form. In 1856 he wrote a famous letter to Joachim:

Sometimes I reflect on the variation form and think that variations should be treated with greater strictness and purity.

The old composers strictly maintained the bass line of the theme, their true theme, throughout.

In Beethoven melody, harmony and rhythm are varied so beautifully.

But I sometimes find that modern composers (the two of us!) tend more to – I don't know the right word – rummage around with the theme. We all stick timidly to the melody, but we don't treat it freely, and really create nothing new from it, but merely encumber it.[236]

Thirteen years later, in a letter to Adolf Schubring, Brahms returned to the same topic, with exactly the same conclusion, except that he was now justifiably aware of the great progress he had made in the technique:

. . . in a theme for variations the main, almost the only, thing that is important to me is the bass line. But that is sacred, it is the firm

foundation on which I build my things . . . If I vary the melody I can hardly do more than be clever or charming, or lend depth, expressive depth, it is true, to a beautiful thought. On top of a given bass, I truly invent something new, I invent new melodies in it, I create.[237]

From the very outset, and throughout his career, variation form was at the heart of Brahms's music. This was not simply because he wrote pieces entitled 'variations', but because it underlies his place in the history of music as well as his method of working and his particular talent. 'Deriving one motif from another,' writes Franz Grasberger, 'developing a theme to the full from a basic motif by means of variation are techniques on which Brahms built up his whole output.'[238] This basic commitment to variation, however, must be taken together with his requirement that it be used to create something new, something truly individual. This also applies to the question of his position within the history of music. He was far from being a composer who merely imitated previous generations. More than anyone else, he achieved the 'organic assimilation of new and old, even very old, material'.[239]

There is one possible misunderstanding that must be cleared up here; there is a clear separation between 'new' works and 'individual' works; 'new' should not simply be seen as a synonym for 'individual'. Brahms's own pessimistic assessment of new developments in music should not obscure the fact that he too opened up new vistas of form. At first sight the determining factor in his music appears to be his clinging to traditional forms. His contemporaries could not see him otherwise, given the clear distance between Brahms's music and that of those whose battle cry was innovation, the dissolution of form. There is no disputing the fact that Brahms clung to classical structures, especially to sonata form. This corresponded to his own personal and artistic search for security; he was afraid of losing his way. But remembering how his often coarse behaviour concealed a highly sensitive person, perhaps it should be intuited that beneath his strict respect for form was a restless nature in search of innovation and change. It was through his understanding of and mastery over form that Brahms renewed it. 'We can say that the result of his experiments with form was the development of a new type which, as the unity of various principles at the highest level, redefined the nature of form.'[240]

Many musicologists have taken up this question. In 1927, Viktor Urbantschitsch wrote of the 'ideal synthesis of variation form and sonata movement'.[241] In 1971, Christian Martin Schmidt summed up these observations by first placing Brahms within the historical context: 'The strictness with which he subordinated musical detail to structural principle is his response to the breakdown of the standard forms which became apparent in the course of the 19th century.' Schmidt's conclusion is that something similar can be seen in the attitude of Brahms the man, namely that 'precisely because the nature of music as a whole was not in question, Brahms was able to focus all his atten-

tion on a problem that composers had certainly been faced with since Bach, namely the problem of how to create, while retaining the same musical substance, so many and varied musical shapes that they fill out a certain period of time in a way that makes sense.'[242]

Arnold Schoenberg was a crucial advocate for the forward drive of Brahms's efforts to extend and, therefore, change the concept of form. In 1895, while Brahms was still alive, Schoenberg was a

Arnold Schoenberg, Brahms' 'heir'

Hans Gál uses the analogy of the seasons: 'A springtime of putting forth shoots and blossom, a summer of massive growth and ripening, an autumn rich in harvest and a winter of gradually diminishing vitality: these are the periods according to which Brahms's work can most readily be classified parallel to his life story.'[247]

It would not be straying too far from the course of Brahms's life to represent the development of his musical output as two curves. The first is characterized by irregular ups and downs, representing the young Brahms's uncertainty, his violent changes of mood; it corresponds roughly to the 'first period', or 'spring', mentioned above. In years, this first graph stretches from 1853, the year in which he met Robert and, in particular, Clara Schumann, to 1867, the year of the *German Requiem*. Or one might extend it further to 1872–73 when he finally settled in Vienna and completed the *Haydn Variations* Op 56, in which he demonstrated his sureness of touch in matters of form. The second curve shows no such irregularities; it rises in a calm, steady line from the famous Piano Quartet Op 60, with its deliberate reference to his 'Werther period' in Düsseldorf, to the *Four Serious Songs* of 1896.

One point in favour of such a broad, sweeping view of Brahms's creative activity is his own usual method of working: he allowed himself – or, rather, his music – time. Although few of his pieces had such a long-drawn-out gestation as his First Symphony, which he completed only after years of hesitation because of the *giant Beethoven*[248] who he sensed at his back, the long time span was closer to the rule for Brahms than an exception. The first movement was completed as early as 1862. 'Recently,' Clara Schumann wrote to Joachim, 'Johannes sent me – just imagine my surprise – the first movement of a symphony with the following bold opening . . .'[249] When Joachim asked Brahms about it, he immediately back-pedalled: *for the time being you'll have to put a ? after*

'*Symph. by J B*'.[250] In 1868 he sent just the horn theme of the finale as a greeting to Clara Schumann; the score was finally completed in 1876.

It really does look as if Brahms, for all his will to succeed and his burning desire to make his mark, knew he would have time. Everything was geared to the long term; even in his musical material, right from the beginning, he showed a preference for expansive melodies and a leaning towards repetition. In his very first recognized work, his C major Piano Sonata Op 1, he made use of the sequence, the transposition of a group of notes or chords to different pitches, an enhanced form of repetition. His use of the variation form also reveals a decided sense of continuity – continuity with tradition and continuity within his own musical output.

SONGS

Brahms called the 49 German Folk Songs WoO33 for voice and piano his *great favourites*.[251] This landmark collection of songs was published in 1894, primarily in response to Brahms's dissatisfaction with the many inferior editions that were being published at that time (although he had actually published a collection of *Children's Songs* WoO 31 himself years earlier, in 1858). The attraction he felt towards folk song is emphasized in a letter to Clara Schumann in which he tells her about the Hamburg Women's

Cover of score of the sixth volume of Brahms's *Lieder* (songs), published by N Simrock, Berlin

Choir (the last volume of WoO33 is for solo voice, piano and choir):

They sang my new German folk songs for me, which they had worked hard to learn.

Now we get together in a very friendly manner one evening a week and I expect the beautiful folk songs will keep me quite pleasantly entertained.

I even think I'll learn something worthwhile, since I'll have to look at and listen to the songs in earnest. I really want to absorb them.

The song is so far off course nowadays that one cannot impress the ideal on one's mind sharply enough. And that's what folk song is for me. [252]

Brahms composed songs throughout his life.[253] He produced 330 songs, including 194 *Lieder* with piano accompaniment, 45 choral compositions and 33 in the two sets of *Liebeslieder,* Op 52 and Op 65. Part of the reason for the rich harvest of vocal music is the fact that this type of musical expression suited him; in his particular case the poetry to be set clearly enhanced his melodic invention. Yet the music still has priority over the words; Brahms never wrote 'programme music' even in his songs. He distinguished between *Lieder* and *Gesänge,* using the first designation for strophic compositions, the second for those that are 'through-composed'. But it was not only folksong, which he caught with such a sure ear, that attracted him to the voice. There are also songs by Brahms, especially for choir, which derive from medieval a cappella music, and many of his strophic *Gesänge* have their origin in his deep knowledge of baroque vocal music. Many different types of canons, all kinds of fugues, counterpoint and complex chromatic gambits were used, and not merely as clever tricks, but as basic components of his composition. Both his own compositional technique and these specialized techniques are completely absorbed into the spirit and feeling of each individual piece.

Brahms's songs are above all 'occasional' works, *pieces d'occasions,* owing their composition to external stimuli, sometimes affairs of the heart. With the *Alto Rhapsody* Op 53, for example, Brahms bade farewell to the hopes he had placed on Julie Schumann – '*Aber abseits, wer ists?*' (But who is this who has turned aside?). There is no place in his output that the key to the relationship between his life and his music is as easy to find as it is in his songs. The presence of the text often appears to make the occasion for the composition easy to deduce; songs can also be given as presents or written with a singer or dedicatee in mind. However, what remains is always an autonomous work of art, even if there were external reasons for its composition, such as when he wrote songs for the repertoire of his Hamburg Women's Choir. Brahms, ever the pragmatist, realized that amateur choirs and the music-making middle classes were the moving forces behind musical culture of his time.

The *Marienlieder* (*Songs to the Virgin Mary*) Op 22 and the motets Op 29, 74 and 110 are among the most outstanding examples of this art. Sometimes the high reputation of Brahms as a composer of 'absolute' music obscures the fact that he composed choral works unequalled in form and expression before or since.

Brahms's songs began with *Liebe und Frühling* (Love and spring) in his Op 3 (composed in 1851), and continued into his late period with songs such as *Feldeinsamkeit* (Meadow solitude) Op 86 no 2 and *Immer leiser wird mein Schlummer* (Ever softer are my slumbers) Op 105 no 2, which represent new high points of his output, as did the *Magelone Romanzen* Op 33 when they first appeared (1865–9). In his old age he returned to the folk song. *I have never scribbled down anything with so much love*, he wrote to Joachim, *indeed, I've fallen head over heels in love with it, and there's no reason why I shouldn't – with something that's not my own.*[254] He has the sense of a wheel coming full circle. *Did you notice*, he asked Clara Schumann after his 49 Folk Songs, the seven volumes of German folk songs with piano accompaniment, appeared in 1894, *that the last of the songs comes in my Opus 1? Did anything strike you about it? It really ought to mean something. It ought to represent the snake biting its own tail, expressing symbolically that the tale is told, the circle closed.*[255] Indeed, just one great, final work was to follow them, another piece for voice, *Four Serious Songs* Op 121.

LARGE-SCALE CHORAL WORKS

Brahms first demonstrated his mastery of large-scale choral form in *A German Requiem* Op 45. With its incredible unity of composition and harmony of words and music, the piece comes as something of a surprise. Until this point Brahms had composed only fairly short choral works, though his practical experience in Detmold and with the Hamburg Women's Choir had helped him make considerable progress in the form. Given the single-mindedness with which the 35-year-old, certainly influenced by Bach and Handel, set such a large-scale work, 'a memorial service whose inner substance is mourning, but also solace,'[256] against all conventional forms of the genre, it must surely be seen as signal of his reaching a state of maturity in his personal life. Furthermore, renunciation is a key theme. This requiem has no reference to salvation or to the Day of Judgment; what determines it is the acceptance of suffering without self-pity. This is the language of the two outer movements, *Selig sind die da Leid tragen* (Blessed are they that mourn) and *Selig sind die Toten* (Blessed are the dead), which can also be heard, only in more concentrated form, in the

Some of the sketches for *A German Requiem*

Four Serious Songs: 'Wherefore I praised the dead, which are already dead, more than the living, which are yet alive.'[257] Brahms repeatedly based his compositions on words from the Bible. In his *Triumphlied (Song of Triumph)* Op 55, the Revelation of St John provided a rather high-flown text for a hymn inspired by the German victory at Sedan in September 1870. Richard Wagner spoke mockingly of a 'fancy-dress concert . . . wearing Handel's hallelujah periwig'[258] with the same combination of accuracy and inaccuracy as most witty remarks. More beautiful and grander are the *Fest- und Gedenksprüche* (*Words of Celebration and Commemoration*) for double choir Op 109. They, too, are filled with patriotic sentiment, but absorbed into a grandiose formal conception. Of course, these were written 18 years after the *Song of Triumph*.

Franco-Prussian War (1870/71)
France's prestige politics and Prussian-German hegemony clashed over the question of Spanish succession. On 19 July 1870 France declared war on Prussia. The Prussian Chancellor Otto von Bismarck (1815–98) persuaded England, Austria and Italy to stay neutral. The German offensive culminated in the battle near the French town of Sedan in September. The French Emperor Napoleon III was taken prisoner. In Paris, besieged by German troops, the Third Republic was proclaimed. Paris surrendered in January. Bismarck used the euphoria in the German states to achieve national unity, engineering the proclamation of the Prussian King as German Emperor Wilhelm I at the same time as the peace treaty was initialled in the French castle of Versailles.

Brahms was exceptionally discriminating in his choice of material; and this was true both of his songs and, even more so, of his choral works. One of his most impressive compositions is the *Schicksalslied (Song of Fate)* Op 54 to lines by the lyric poet Friedrich Hölderlin (1770–1843), completed in 1870. It is, moreover, a particularly characteristic example of Brahms's treatment of words, showing clearly how setting the words was an essential starting point for the composition, but nothing more than that. Brahms even continued the poem in the music by returning it to the world of the gods, transposed, after the struggles of mortal men. *You see, I'm saying something the poet doesn't say.*[259] The result is that the musical end of the work is not the gnawing uncertainty of Hölderlin's text: 'Blind, suffering humanity/ Thrown, hour to hour/ From cliff to cliff/ like water:/ Down the years: into the uncertain depths.' Instead Brahms's setting moves into a light that does not exclude hope. Music, without violating the text, is the decisive factor.

The choral works, and the *German Requiem* in particular, are repeated essays with large forces. The resolve to work with large forces was one that came early to Brahms. When Robert Schumann wrote that he should listen to the openings of Beethoven's symphonies and try to do something similar, it was the spirit of the 19th century speaking through him, a century with a predilection for the monumental. Had it not been for the demands made on him by contemporary society, there would probably not have been any large-scale orchestral works, to say nothing of symphonies, by Brahms.

ORCHESTRAL WORKS

It was a struggle for Brahms to master orchestral technique, the use of large forces. He was, first and foremost, a pianist, and the inward looking nature of his emotional language did not lend itself to grand public statements without struggle. Even at the time of publication of the Double Concerto, in 1888, he could still write to Clara Schumann, *It's a different matter writing for instruments you only know at second hand – which you can only hear with your mind's ear, so to speak – and writing for an instrument you know through and through, as I know the piano, where I know precisely what I'm writing and why I'm writing it in that particular way.*[260]

By that time, of course, he was quite the master of writing for the orchestra. At the beginning, however, things were quite different. For all the unmistakable 'Brahms sound' of the two orchestral serenades, to a degree they must be regarded as practice pieces. To identify the true beginnings of his orchestral music, the piece that automatically comes to mind is the key work of his early period, the First Piano Concerto. Brahms worked on the concerto for four years. Originally conceived as a sonata for two pianos, it was to become his first important orchestral work. Comparison with the Second Piano Concerto, published 22 years later, makes its lack of balance particularly clear, but what a magnificent lack of balance! The first movement, which never quite manages to attain the monumental idea behind it, is the moving expression of a young man who was finding it difficult to come to terms with his own life. It is surely not over-interpretation to see in this concerto, and in its first movement in particular, the reflection of his troubled passion for Clara Schumann, a reflection that can still be glimpsed in the First Symphony, published in 1877, the reason being that the initial ideas for the latter work go so far back.

Brahms took his time over his First Symphony. He also made great demands on his audience, initially, as always, his friends; this first symphony has a severity that makes it not easily accessible. Brahms realized this: *And I'd like to add the presumably very surprising news that my symphony is long and not exactly lovable.*[261] It is difficult for the listeners of today to put themselves in the place of the first audience for a work that now seems pleasantly, if dangerously, familiar. One thing that contributes to its greatness and to its popularity today, despite its complex structure, is that the First Symphony has an extraordinarily unified musical idiom. It was more difficult for Brahms's contemporaries. Theodor Billroth wrote, 'Despite all their energy and passion, I cannot warm to the themes of the first movement, rhythmically they are very long-winded and harmonically too defiantly severe, even if they do have a yearning that stirs you . . .'[262] Billroth has perceived something at first hearing that doesn't only apply to the First Symphony. His remark that he could 'not warm to the themes of the first movement' is interesting only for its immediacy of response, perhaps difficult for today's audience; but with 'defiance' and 'yearning' he hit on two of the defining characteristics of Brahms's music. Even the D major Second Symphony Opus 73, sometimes referred to as his 'Pastoral' (one of the group of works that was produced in the three summers – 1877, 1878 and 1879 – that he spent in Pörtschach), can be seen as carefree and untouched by 'defiance' and 'yearning' only at the most superficial acquaintance. Whatever the apparent surface of the work, it is the most poetic of his four symphonies. And yet there is a huge difference between the First and Second symphonies, in fact, between the first and all three others. In the First, Brahms's struggle with his personal life is clearly visible in the music. By contrast, the other symphonies are evidence of a completed development; his personal defiance has been transformed into firmness, whereas his yearning has been increasingly transformed into a yearning for lost hope, into resignation.

During the time he was writing the Second Symphony in 1877, little of the more muted tone of the First was apparent. The two great D major works, the Second Symphony and the Violin Concerto that followed it, are both imbued with a feeling of joyous exhilaration, which is somewhat unusual for Brahms.

The Violin Concerto Op 77, like all other pieces before it, was changed again and again, in response to Brahms's almost insatiable desire for perfection of form and expression. This process was conducted primarily through discussion with Joachim, to whom the concerto is dedicated. Joachim had been involved in the questions concerning Brahms's orchestral style from the very start, particularly with regard to the First Serenade Op 11, which

Joachim called the 'Symphony-Serenade'. Brahms was still working on it after the initial performances. *I want to go through it with a less talented violinist than you, since I fear you aren't being bold or strict enough. The only way you'll impress me is with a lot of suggestions and changes.*[263] Brahms did not write the cadenza that traditionally comes at the end of the first movement. He felt that virtuoso music like that, which touched the very limits of violin technique, was beyond him. His was the last major concerto where the composer preserved the classical tradition of leaving the cadenza to the soloist, even though there is a measure of choice, in say, the Khachaturian Concerto. *Joachim played my piece more beautifully with every rehearsal, and by the time the concert came his cadenza was so splendid the people clapped right on into my coda.*[264]

When Brahms came to write his Second Piano Concerto Op 83, it is as if he were keeping a promise he had made himself. After the first had flopped at its Leipzig premiere, he wrote *A second will certainly sound different.*[265] So it proved. The calm control of this work is striking after the passionate restlessness of the first, which was born out of his time of crisis. Here his sureness of touch in handling the orchestration, refined and proved through the fires of two preceding symphonies and the violin concerto, and the solo instrument was no longer in doubt. Moreover, the solo instrument, the piano, was the one instrument that he knew *through and through*.[266] The expression 'symphony with piano obbligato', repeatedly 'reinvented' since Mozart and Beethoven, sometimes in a positive and sometimes in a negative sense, fits this piece as no other. In sharp contrast to the First Concerto, the piano is now truly integrated, while still first among equals. During this time Brahms must surely have found his own productivity very enjoyable. For once, he wrote about his work with satisfaction, even if he tried to play it down with a bantering tone: *I've just rather rashly dashed off a lovely big piano concerto without first asking whether there might be a woman who would*

run away from her husband for its sake! And now I'm stuck here –
with the child in my lap and no one to suckle or play it. And to crown
it all there's a Scherzo in it of such tenderness, such fragrance . . .
Another of my intentions with this piece was to show how the artist must
divest himself of all passion so he can be transported into pure ethereal
realms.[267]

The B flat major Piano Concerto and the Third Symphony Op
90, which was completed two years after the Second in 1833, are
the high points of formal balance in Brahms's output. They can
be described as his 'classical' works and are possessed of a unity
that can be achieved only by a composer who has 'divested himself of all passion'. Despite the artfully generated dramatic cli-
maxes, these are large-scale works with a strong sense of
continuity, with space for reflection and contemplation. The Third
Symphony demands comparison with works of architecture; the
component parts of a spacious and complete construction are made
visible in a truly classical manner.

The Fourth Symphony Op 98 in E minor was composed in
1884–5 and is closely related to the Third. In this work, som-
brely dramatic elements have a greater role, the exhilarating sense
of forward movement is banished forever. There was no way back,
and there was no way forward, either. The feeling of retrospec-
tion is so strong that it is perhaps only logical that there no further symphonies followed this one. In this Fourth Symphony
Brahms's very individual approach to music was once more displayed: commitment to tradition and renewal through assimilation are combined with the constant forward momentum of
'thematic processes'. The 31 variations of the last movement are
nothing short of a musical miracle; this movement, of course,
was Brahms's titanic response to his encounter with Bach's
'Chaconne' for solo violin, Joseph Joachim's 'signature work'. As
Brahms said to Siegfried Ochs, *What would you think of a sym-*
phonic movement based on this theme sometime?[268]

The Double Concerto in A minor Op 102 for Violin and Cello appeared two years after the Fourth Symphony. Brahms wrote it for his friend Joseph Joachim as a token of reconciliation after a long silence, which had been occasioned by Brahms's insensitive behaviour in the matter of Joachim's divorce. Once again, he did not express this in words, but hoped he would be understood through his music: *I do not say out loud and in words what I silently hope and wish for.*[269] But even the experts within Brahms's circle could not understand the piece, and today this powerful work still arouses a degree of incomprehension. Part of the reason may lie in the unusual combination of solo violin and cello. Even here, though, Brahms was looking back to an older form, namely the classical *sinfonia concertante*, which had been brought to its apogee by Mozart and Haydn. He moulded this to suit his purposes, and not only succeeded in writing a frequently remarked upon lyrical Andante, but came closer than ever before to making two instruments in dialogue speak with one voice so that 'something unique comes about, the merging of chamber music, concerto and symphony.'[270] The ramifications of this concerto are still being felt, influencing composers as diverse as Tippett, Rihm and Schnittke in the late 20th century revival of this form.

PIANO AND CHAMBER MUSIC

Brahms began his musical life writing for the piano and piano pieces occupied his final years. This was not by chance: he loved this kind of retrospective view just as he loved introducing echoes of earlier composers. Brahms, as a pianist, began as a composer of piano music with, in order of composition, a Scherzo Op 4, the Sonata in F sharp minor Op 2, the Sonata in C major Op 1 and the large-scale Piano Sonata in F minor Op 5. After this last piece, which was written in 1853, Brahms, in a striking way that was typical of him, wrote no more piano sonatas. He had got as much as he could out of the form, which, even as early as 1853, could scarcely be bettered in its contrapuntal working out. Listening to these sonatas immediately makes one realize that Robert Schumann's enthusiastic article 'New Paths' was no exaggeration.

Brahms later put sonata form to the test again in his concertos and symphonies, and the sonata was also revived in a new form in his late chamber music. Although he did not write any more piano sonatas, the piano is a strong and sometimes dominant partner in the sonatas for violin, cello and clarinet. Brahms was one of the last composers to preserve the classical Viennese notion of the 'accompanied' sonata, which had been innovated by C P E Bach, and perfected by Beethoven, where the solo piano is 'accompanied' by a melody instrument. All of his duo sonatas conform to this model (as is made clear on the title page of the F major Sonata Op 99 of 1887,'for piano and cello') even when, such as in the Op 78 *Regenlied* Sonata with Violin, the melodic imperative is primarily with the 'accompanying' partner.

As early as 1853, after the F minor Sonata, Brahms knew that he had nothing left to 'prove' at the piano, certainly not that he was a 'successor' to anyone. From that point on his piano music became the intimate setting for a personal examination of various aspects of music: the variation technique, the 'ballade', studies in character and atmosphere, *intermezzi* of great artistry, sometimes rhythmically complex and very chromatic, and occasionally with the lightness of a waltz. It is perhaps in his piano music that we can most clearly see 'Brahms from the inside', and 'Brahms the progressive'. 'When Brahms asked the pianist to play duplets or quadruplets with one hand while the other was playing triplets,' Schoenberg wrote in 1946, 'people did not like it and said it made them feel seasick. Yet that was presumably the beginning of the polyrhythmic structure of many contemporary scores.'[271] Indeed, as has been said many times, of all composers,

Brahms is the one who most anticipated the complex rhythmic overlayerings of the 20th century, a composer whose metric innovations were not surpassed until Stravinsky, and who actually looks forward as far as the techniques employed by living composers such as Ligeti.

What has already been said about Brahms as a composer who renewed and extended musical forms, the sheer breadth of his enormous range of expression can be seen in his chamber music. To Brahms, who loved the transparency of this form, and never quite overcame his inhibitions vis-à-vis large audiences, who regarded the effect of large-scale forces almost as 'giving in' to popular taste, chamber music was the one genre that best suited his talents. The course of his musical and personal development can be followed through his chamber music. The B major Piano Trio Op 8, for example, characterizes Brahms's life and work as no other. Its origin lies in the confusing, inspiring relationship with the Schumanns; the original version from 1854 already contains 'the whole Brahms' and he, forever looking back and reviewing his work, took it up again in 1891 to give it its final shape. This exercise turned out to be a complete reworking, yet one that retained essential elements of the first version of 1854, without any stylistic incongruities. After 36 years, with the sure touch of the mastery he had since attained, Brahms was able to recapture the expression of this youthful work. The Trio is also important for a further reason: in its early version it was the first work of more than one movement in which Brahms grappled with sonata form.

Schoenberg was fascinated by Brahms's chamber music. Remarkably he arranged the G minor Piano Quartet Op 25 for large orchestra. He wrote:

'My reasons:

1. I like this piece.

2. It is seldom played.

3. It is always very badly played, because the better the pianist,

the louder he plays and you hear nothing from the strings. I wanted to hear everything for once, and this I achieved.

My intentions:

1. To remain strictly in the style of Brahms and not to go farther than he himself would have gone if he lived today.

2. To watch carefully all those laws that Brahms obeyed and not to violate [any of those] that are only known to musicians educated in his environment.'[272]

With his B flat major String Quartet Op 67, written in 1875, Brahms seems to have taken the decisive step in extending this form. 'While there are two contrasting themes in the first movement, their polarity is derived from musical *elements*.'[273] Clara Schumann was deeply moved by the *Adagio*. Brahms wrote to her: *Such an Adagio, only a German can compose, for only his deeply serious eye can still look forth full of love amidst great suffering.*[274] This development is pursued consistently right up to the Clarinet Quintet Op 115, composed in 1891. Brahms may have been sketching out a similar quintet three years earlier, as letters that he exchanged with Clara Schumann at this time make reference to a 'fierce' (*grausame*) quintet in E minor. The impulse behind the latter composition came from Brahms's acquaintance with the clarinettist Richard Mühlfeld, *absolutely the best wind player I know.*[275] One could therefore call this another 'occasional piece', which provides Brahms with

Brahms memorial on the Karlsplatz in Vienna

the occasion to again demonstrate his complete mastery of form. This form might be considered to have reached its culmination with Mozart's Clarinet Quintet, but the later work, with its almost otherworldly beauty, seems to follow on from it quite naturally.

Chamber music, a form that must have come almost instinctively to the introverted Brahms, is the one that, despite the breathtaking symphonies and his vocal music, bears the deepest impression of his creative, artistic intentions and feelings.

It probably also contained, through what Karl Dahlhaus called the 'process of developing variation',[276] the strongest innovative power, given that it was chamber music, rather than symphonic writing, that played the central role in the transition to atonality. It would be nice to be able to finish off with a quotation from Brahms explaining his chamber music, but since his reserve and reticence stopped him talking much

Brahms's late collaboration with the clarinettist Richard Mühlfeld (1856–1907) proved to be one of the richest musical relationships of his composing life, resulting in four chamber works that stand at the pinnacle of his output. Like Mozart and Stadler, Brahms's late clarinet works were inspired by the playing of a particular clarinettist. In the spring of 1891, Brahms requested that Mühlfeld play a private recital for him, and quizzed him about his technique. This directly inspired the Trio Op 114 and the masterly Quintet Op 115. Brahms described Mühlfeld as '*Fräulein Klarinette*'. Mühlfeld originally trained as a violinist and played in the Meinigen Court Theatre before teaching himself the clarinet. In 1876 he was appointed the first clarinet of the *Saxe-Meinigen Hofkapelle*, where he played under Hans von Bülow. He was the first clarinettist of the Bayreuth Festival from 1884–96. Clara Schumann described his playing as 'at once delicate, warm and affected, and at the same time showing the most perfect technique'. The two Sonatas Op 120 that Brahms wrote for his *dear nightingale* at Bad Ischl in the summer of 1894 are still unsurpassed in either the woodwind or any other repertoire.

about his works, there is nothing left but to repeat his statement, *I speak through my music.*[277]

Johannes Brahms.

Notes

1 Eugenie Schumann, *Memoirs*, tr Marie Busch (London, 1985)

2 Samuel Taylor Coleridge, *Kubla Khan*

3 Florence May, *The Life of Brahms* vol. 1 (1905; reprint, Neptune City, New Jersey, 1981), pp 128–9.

4 Catalogue, in *Fine printed and manuscript music – Sothebys – Entry 25* (reprint, London): December 1997).

5 Jan Swafford, *Johannes Brahms* (reprint, London) 1999), pp 457–9.

6 Karl Wörner, *Das Zeitalter der thematischen Prozesse* (Regensburg, 1969).

7 Albrecht Dümling (ed), *Verteidigung des musikalischen Fortschritts. Brahms und Schoenberg* (Hamburg, 1990), p 9.

8 Quoted from: Max Kalbeck, *Johannes Brahms*, 4 vols (Tutzing, 1976), vol 1, p 152.

9 Wilfrid Mellers,*The Sonata Principle* (London, 1959), p 18.

10 Mellers, p 44.

11 Mellers, p 53.

12 Kalbeck, vol 1, p 165.

13 Kalbeck, vol 2, p 350.

14 Johannes Brahms: *Life and Letters*, selected and anno- tated by Styra Avins, tr Josef Eisinger and Styra Avins (Oxford/New York, 1997), p 660. (In later refer- ences as *L&L.*)

15 Kalbeck, vol 4, p 154.

16 Claude Rostand, *Brahms* (Paris, 1978), p 27

17 Johannes Brahms: *Briefwechsel*, 4 vols, reprint (Tutzing, 1974). (In later references as *Briefwechsel*)

18 Hans Gál, *Johannes Brahms. His Work and Personality*, tr Joseph Stein (London, 1963), p 26.

19 Richard Specht, *Johannes Brahms*, tr Eric Blom (London and Toronto; New York, 1930), p 287.

20 Albert Dietrich, J V Widmann, *Recollections of Johannes Brahms*, tr Dora E Hecht (London, 1899), p 122.

21 Kalbeck, vol 4, p 518f.

22 Klaus Groth, 'Notizen Über Johannes Brahms', quoted in *Briefe der Freundschaft. Johannes Brahms-Klaus Groth*, ed Volquart Pauls (Heide, 1956).

23 Kalbeck, vol 1, p 4f.

24 Kalbeck, vol 1, p 16.

25 Kalbeck, vol 1, p 21f.

26 May, p 69

27 Brahms to Hermann Deiters

28 May, vol 1, p 35
29 Brahms to Julius Allgeyer (Vienna, 18 Mar 1876), *L&L*, pp 491–2.
30 Brahms to Julius Allgeyer (Apr or May 1895), *L&L*, p 725.
31 Dietrich/Widmann, p 188.
32 Franz Grasberger, *Johannes Brahms. Variationen um sein Wesen* (Vienna, 1952), p 137.
33 E T A Hoffmann: *Fantasiestücke in Callots Manier. III Kreisleriana* in *Sämtliche Werke* vol 2/1 (Frankfurt/M, 1993), pp 32–3.
34 Ricarda Huch, *Die Romantik* (Tübingen, 1951), p 112f.
35 For Brahms's will, see Kalbeck, vol 4, p 227ff.
36 Kalbeck, vol 1, p 62.
37 Kalbeck, vol 1, p 59f.
38 Kalbeck, vol 1, p 74.
39 Kalbeck, vol 1, p 79.
40 Kalbeck, vol 1, p 90.
41 Kalbeck, vol 1, p 90.
42 Brahms to Joachim (Weimar, 29 Jun 1853), *L&L*, p 12.
43 Brahms to Joachim (Düsseldorf, 26 Feb 1856), *L&L,* 123–4.
44 Brahms to Joachim (Düsseldorf, 27 Apr 1856), *L&L,* 128.
45 Brahms to Joachim (Düsseldorf, Jun 1856), *L&L*, p 137.
46 Joachim to Brahms, quoted in *L&L*, p 555.
47 Brahms to Joachim (Ischl, 27 Jul 1880), *L&L*, p 571.
48 Brahms to Amalie Joachim (Dec 1880), *L&L*, p 572.
49 Ibid.
50 Brahms to Joachim (Düsseldorf, beginning of Oct 1853), *L&L*, p 21.
51 Robert Schumann to Hermann Härtel (Düsseldorf, 8 Oct 1853), quoted in Kalbeck, vol 1, p 123.
52 Robert Schumann, 'New Paths', May vol 1 pp 131–2; also in Specht pp 363–4.
53 Brahms to Robert Schumann (Hanover, 16 Nov 1853); *L&L*, p 24; also in *Letters of Clara Schumann and Johannes Brahms 1853–1896*, ed Berthold Litzmann, 2 vols (London, 1927), vol 1, p 1. (In later references as *CS-JB*'.)
54 Conversation with Max Kalbeck, Kalbeck, vol 1, p 138.
55 'Weary Hour' in Thomas Mann, *Stories of Three Decades*, tr H T Lowe-Porter (London, 1936), p 293.
56 Conversation with Richard Heuberger, in Grasberger, p 119.
57 Brahms to Robert Schumann (Hanover, 29 Nov 1853), *L&L*, p 27; *CS-JB*, vol 1, p 2.
58 Julius Otto Grimm to Joachim (Düsseldorf, 9 Apr 1854), *L&L*, p 42.
59 Brahms to Joachim (Düsseldorf, May 1854), *Briefwechsel*, vol 5, p 40.
60 Quoted in Eva Weissweiler, *Clara Schumann. Eine*

Biographie (Hamburg, 1990), p 290.

61 *Clara Schumann – Johannes Brahms. Briefe aus den Jahren 1853–1896*, 2 vols, ed Berthold Litzmann (Leipzig 1927), (in later references as *CS-JB Briefe*), vol 1, p 7.

62 Brahms to Clara Schumann (Eßlingen, 15 Aug 1854), *L&L*, p 51; *CS-JB*, vol 1, p 6.

63 Brahms to Clara Schumann (Ulm, 16 Aug, 1854), *L&L*, p 52–3; *CS-JB*, vol 1, pp 7–8.

64 Brahms to Clara Schumann (Düsseldorf, 27 Aug, 1854), *L&L*, p 61; *CS-JB*, vol 1, p 12.

65 Brahms to Clara Schumann (Hamburg, 21 Oct 1854), *L&L*, p 66; *CS-JB*, vol 1, p 14.

66 Brahms to Clara Schumann (Hamburg, 25 Nov 1854), *L&L*, p 69.

67 Brahms to Clara Schumann (Hamburg, 8 Dec 1854), *L&L*, p 75.

68 Brahms to Clara Schumann (Hamburg, 15 Dec 1854), *L&L*, pp 79–80; *CS-JB*, vol 1, pp 20–21.

69 Brahms to Clara Schumann (Düsseldorf, 25 Jan 1855), *CS-JB*, vol 1, p 23.

70 Brahms to Clara Schumann (Düsseldorf, 3 Feb 1855), *L&L*, p 85.

71 Brahms to Clara Schumann (Düsseldorf, 23 Jun 1855), *CS-JB*, vol 1, p 39.

72 Brahms to Clara Schumann (Düsseldorf, 19 Aug 1855),

CS-JB, vol 1, p 46.

73 Brahms to Clara Schumann (Hamburg, 4 Dec 1855), *CS-JB*, vol 1, p 58.

74 Brahms to Clara Schumann (Hanover, 21 Dec 1859), *CS-JB Briefe*, vol 1, p 290.

75 Clara Schumann to Brahms (Düsseldorf, 16 May 1856), *CS-JB Briefe*, vol 1, p 186.

76 Brahms to Clara Schumann (Düsseldorf, 24 May 1856); *L&L*, p 133; *CS-JB*, vol 1, p 72. The first sentence is a quotation from Brahms's own previous letter of 16 May, which he is here explaining, at the same time going over from the 'Sie' form of address to 'Du'.

77 Brahms to Clara Schumann (Düsseldorf, 31 May 1856), *L&L*, p 134; *CS-JB*, vol 1, p 73.

78 Brahms to Julius Otto Grimm (Heidelberg, Sep 1856), *L&L*, p 142.

79 Brahms to Theodor Billroth (23 Oct 1874), Otto Gottlieb Billroth, *Brahms und Billroth im Briefwechsel*, Berlin, 1991, p 210. (In later references as *Brahms und Billroth*.)

80 Johann Wolfgang von Goethe, *The Sorrows of Young Werther*, tr Catherine Hutter (New York, 1962), p 127.

81 Gál, p 94.

82 The F minor Sonata Op 5 (1853), the B major Trio Op 8 (1854), the Ballades for piano Op 10 (1854) and the Songs Op 6 and 7. A quartet that Joachim looked

through for him in the spring of 1856 can no longer be identified with any certainty.

83 Kalbeck, vol 1, p 255.

84 Brahms to Clara Schumann (4 Dec 1855), *CS-JB*, vol 1 p 57.

85 Brahms to Barthold Senff (Hamburg, 26 Dec 1853), *L&L*, p 31. The sonata in question is the F minor Sonata, Op 5.

86 Dietrich/Widmann, pp 2–4.

87 Brahms to Clara Schumann (Hamburg, 28 Oct 1856), *CS-JB*, vol 1, p 193.

88 Brahms to Clara Schumann (Detmold, 11 Oct 1857), *L&L*, p 157; *CS-JB*, vol 1, p 78.

89 See Willi Schramm, *Johannes Brahms in Detmold* (Leipzig, 1933).

90 Brahms to Joachim (Detmold, 5 Dec 1857), *L&L*, p 161.

91 See Schramm, p 28.

92 See Schramm, p 34.

93 Brahms to Joachim (Düsseldorf, 1 Apr 1854), *Briefwechsel*, vol 5, p 191; (*L&L*, p 41, fn 19 refers).

94 Ibid.

95 The young musicians in Schumann's circle had given him the title 'Dominus'. Cp Brahms addressing him as 'Mynheer Domine' in the letter of 29 Nov 1853, (quoted p 38, fn 57).

96 Brahms to Joachim (Düsseldorf, 11 Jul 1857), *Briefwechsel*, vol 5, p 186f.

97 Brahms to Joachim (Detmold, 22 Dec 1857), *Briefwechsel*, vol 5, p 195f.

98 Brahms to Joachim (Leipzig, 28 Jan 1859), *L&L*, pp 188–90.

99 'Der Kuß' (The Kiss), Brahms Op 19, no 1.

100 Brahms to Grimm (Detmold, Oct/Nov 1858), *L&L*, pp 177–8.

101 Schramm, p 36.

102 Brahms to Marie Schumann (Vienna, Apr 1896), *L&L*, p 732.

103 Brahms to Agathe von Siebold (1859), in Richard Litterscheid, *Johannes Brahms in seinen Schriften und Briefen*, Berlin, 1943, p 50.

104 Clara Schumann to Brahms (Amsterdam, 5 Feb 1860), *CS–JB Briefe*, vol 1, pp 295–298.

105 Brahms to Auguste Brandt and Bertha Porubsky (Detmold, 9 Oct 1859), *L&L*, p 202.

106 In German notation 'H' = 'B' (and 'B' = 'B flat').

107 Karl Geiringer *Brahms. His Life and Work*, tr H B Weiner and Bernard Miall (London, 2nd revised and enlarged edition, 1948), p 60.

108 Gál, p 96.

109 Brahms to Fräulein von Meysenburg (1859), May, vol 1, p 258.

110 The *Avertimento* is given in May, vol 1, pp 273–4.

111 Brahms to Friedchen Wagner (Detmold, Sep 1859), *L&L*, p 201.

112 Brahms to Clara Schumann

113 Kalbeck, vol 1, p 435f.

114 Goethe, *Torquato Tasso*, (Act 1, Sc 3)

115 Brahms to Joachim (Hamburg, Dec 1860), *L&L*, p 227.

116 Brahms to Rieter-Biedermann (Nov 1958), Litterscheid, p 196.

117 Brahms to Rieter-Biedermann (Hamburg, 29 Aug 1860), Litterscheid, p 198.

118 Brahms to Rieter-Biedermann (Hamburg, 29 Aug 1860), Litterscheid, p 198.

119 Brahms to Clara Schumann (Hamburg, 11 Sep 1860), Litterscheid, p 202.

120 Brahms to Joachim (Hamburg, 13 Sep 1860), *L&L*, p 226.

121 Brahms to Clara Schumann (Detmold, 9 Nov 1859), *CS-JB*, vol 1, p 112.

122 Berthold Litzmann, *Clara Schumann: An Artist's Life. Based on material found in diaries and letters*, 2 vols, tr Grace E Hadow (London/Leipzig, 1913), vol 2, pp 200–201.

123 Brahms to Joachim (Hamburg, 18 Jun 1859), *Briefwechsel*, vol 5, p 246ff.

124 The sketches for his A major Piano Quartet.

125 Dietrich/Widmann, pp 37–8.

126 Kalbeck, vol 1, p 462 fn.

127 Brahms to Breitkopf & Härtel (Hamm, 14 Apr 1862), *L&L*, pp 244–5.

128 May, vol 1, p 304.

129 Brahms to Julius Otto Grimm (Vienna, Nov 1862), *L&L*, p 248.

130 Kalbeck, vol 2, p 18.

131 Brahms to his parents (Vienna, 30 Nov 1862), *L&L*, p 260.

132 Kalbeck, vol 2, p 38.

133 Joachim to Theodor Avé-Lallement (31 Jan 1863), *L&L*, p 266.

134 Brahms to Clara Schumann (Vienna, 18 Nov 1862), *L&L*, p 258; May, vol 1, p 149.

135 Brahms to Adolf Schubring (Vienna, 26 Mar 1863), *L&L*, p 276.

136 Brahms to the committee of the Vienna Singakademie (30 May 1863), *L&L*, p 281.

137 Specht, pp 137–8.

138 Eduard Hanslick on the Singakademie's concert of 6 Jan 1864; May, vol 2, p 349.

139 May, vol 1, pp 2–3.

140 May, vol 1, p 4.

141 May, vol 1, pp 9–10, 11–12, 17.

142 May, vol 1, p 18.

143 Brahms to Rieter-Biedermann (Vienna, 18 Feb 1863), *L&L*, pp 274–5.

144 Kalbeck, vol 3, p 71.

145 Brahms to Hanslick (May 1884), *L&L*, pp 612–13.

146 Brahms to Hanslick (May 1884), *L&L*, p 614.

147 Specht, p 172.

148 Specht, p 173.

149 Kalbeck, vol 2, p 418.

(3 Jul 1859), *CS-JB*, vol 1, pp 105–6.

150   Elisabet von Herzogenberg to Brahms (20 Oct 1885), in: *Johannes Brahms: The Herzogenberg Correspondence*, ed Max Kalbeck, tr Hannah Bryant (London, 1909), p 257. (In future references as *Herzogenberg*.)

151   Elisabet von Herzogenberg to Brahms (10 Mar 1878), *Herzogenberg*, pp 50–51.

152   Kalbeck, vol 3, p 7.

153   Elisabet von Herzogenberg to Brahms (1 Mar 1878), *Herzogenberg*, p 47.

154   Brahms to Elisabet von Herzogenberg (Nov 1879), *Herzogenberg*, p 90.

155   Brahms to Elisabet von Herzogenberg (3 Nov 1888), *Herzogenberg*, p 364.

156   Kalbeck, vol 1, p 63.

157   Kalbeck, vol 1, p 166.

158   Specht, p 236.

159   Specht, p 237.

160   Specht, p 236.

161   Brahms to his father (Vienna, 30 Apr 1869), *L&L*, pp 391–2.

162   Brahms to Karl Reinthaler (Vienna, 30 Apr 1869), *Briefwechsel,* vol 3, p 17.

163   Brahms to the music publisher, Berthold Senff (Vienna, 20 Jan 1869), Litterscheid, p 285.

164   Fritz Simrock to Brahms (Berlin, 22 Feb 1873), Kurt Stephenson, *Johannes Brahms und Fritz Simrock. Weg einer Freundschaft* (Hamburg, 1961), p 57.

165   Brahms to Fritz Simrock (Preßbaum, 19 Sep 1881), *L&L*, p 584.

166   Brahms to Fritz Simrock (Tutzing, 31 May 1873), *Briefwechsel*, vol 9, p 142.

167   Brahms to Fritz Simrock (Preßbaum, 19 Sep 1881), *L&L*, p 585.

168   Stephenson, p 57.

169   Specht, p 246.

170   Kalbeck, vol 3, p 311.

171   Specht, p 246.

172   Brahms to Ferdinand Hiller (Oct 1881), *L&L*, pp 581–2.

173   Kalbeck, vol 3, p 311.

174   Litzmann, vol 2, p 362.

175   Kalbeck, vol 3, p 307.

176   Kalbeck, vol 3, p 314.

177   Kalbeck, vol 3, p 312.

178   Kalbeck, vol 3, p 313.

179   Kalbeck, vol 4, p 267.

180   Grasberger, p 154.

181   Litterscheid, p 143.

182   Litterscheid, p 143.

183   Brahms to Billroth (Dec 1876), *L&L*, p 506.

184   *Herzogenberg*, pp 127–8.

185   Kalbeck, vol 3, p 247; quoted in Specht, pp 306–7.

186   Kalbeck, vol 3, p 247.

187   Litzmann, vol 2, p 268.

188   Billroth to Brahms (Vienna, 23 Feb 1885), *Brahms und Billroth*, p 370.

189   Brahms to Regierungsrat H Steinmetz of Düsseldorf (15 Oct 1876); quoted from the original in the possession of the Heinrich Heine Institute of the Düsseldorf Museum.

190   Brahms to Steinmetz.

191   Leaflet of 2 Dec 1867; quoted from copy in the Heinrich Heine Institute, Düsseldorf Museum.

192   Specht, p 314.

193   Specht, German edition,

p 340.

194 Brahms to Fritz Simrock (Vienna, 8 May 1896), *L&L*, p 733; also in Specht, p 348.

195 Silhouette by Otto Böhler. The Red Hedgehog was a restaurant Brahms frequented.

196 Bostein, p 205.

197 Specht, p 350.

198 Specht, p 356.

199 Kalbeck, vol 1, p 115 (in 1st ed of 1904).

200 Gál, pp 33–4.

201 Brahms to Joachim (Hamburg, 7 Aug 1859), *L&L*, pp 196–7.

202 Specht, pp 87–8.

203 Kalbeck, vol 1, p 204 (in first edition of 1904).

204 Kalbeck, vol 2, p 117.

205 Richard Wagner, 'Über das Dirigieren', *Neue Zeitschrift für Musik,* 1869.

206 Groth.

207 Wagner to Brahms, (Bayreuth, 6 Jun 1875), *L&L*, p 476.

208 Brahms to Wagner (nr Heidelberg, Jun 1875), *L&L*, pp 476–7.

209 Wagner to Brahms (Bayreuth, 26 Jun 1875), *L&L*, p 478.

210 Brahms to Wagner (Jun 1875), *L&L*, p 479.

211 Brahms to Bülow (1882).

212 Kalbeck, vol 2, p 125.

213 Clara Schumann to Brahms (Wiesbaden, 1 Jul 1858), *CS-JB*, vol 1, pp 86–7.

214 Walter Deppisch, *Richard Strauss*, Reinbek, 1968, p 33.

215 Specht, p 240.

216 Specht, p 239.

217 Specht, p 262, reports this as coming from a conversation with Brahms in the year of his death.

218 Josef Müller-Marein, Hannes Reichardt, *Das musikalische Selbstporträt* (Hamburg, 1963), p 50.

219 A remark for which there is only anecdotal evidence.

220 Brahms to Joachim (Vienna, May 1879), *L&L*, p 549, commentating on Dvořak's Serenade for Wind Op 44.

221 Gál, p 151.

222 Kalbeck, vol 3, p 411.

223 Hugo Wolf review of 27 Apr 1884, quoted in Kalbeck, vol 3, p 412.

224 Review in the *Neue Berliner Musikzeitung*, 1859, vol 13, no 26, quoted in Carl Dahlhaus, *Johannes Brahms Klavierkonzert Nr. 1 d-moll, op. 15*, Munich, 1965.

225 Brahms to Clara Schumann (11 Oct 1857), *L&L*, p 159; *CS-JB*, vol 1, p 79.

226 Specht, p 353.

227 Paul Bekker, *Gustav Mahler's Sinfonien* (Berlin 1921), quoted from Wolfgang Schreiber, *Gustav Mahler* (Reinbek, 1971), p 128.

228 Brahms to Clara Schumann (Düsseldorf, 31 May 1856), *L&L*, p 136; *CS-JB*, vol 1, p 74.

229 Kalbeck, vol 3, p 109 fn.

230 Kalbeck, vol 1, p 160.

231 Brahms to Bülow (Mürzzuschlag, Oct 1884), *L&L*, p 617.

232 Kalbeck, vol 2, p 178.

233 Brahms in conversation with Georg Henschel, reported in Kalbeck vol 2, pp 178f.

234 Brahms to Clara Schumann (Switzerland, Sep 1868), *L&L*, p 366, *CS-JB*, vol 2, p 229.

235 Brahms to Clara Schumann (Düsseldorf, 21 Aug 1854), *L&L*, p 55; *CS-JB*, vol 1, p 8.

236 Brahms to Joachim (Düsseldorf, Jun 1856), *L&L*, p 138.

237 Brahms to Adolf Schubring (Vienna, 16 Feb 1869), *L&L*, pp 383–4.

238 Grasberger, p 55.

239 August Sturke, *Der Stil in Johannes Brahms' Werken*, Würzburg, 1932.

240 Klaus Stahmer, *Musikalische Formung in soziologischem Bezug. Dargestellt an der instrumentalen Kammermusik von Johannes Brahms*, dissertation (Kiel, 1968), p 185.

241 Viktor Urbantschitsch, *Die Entwicklung der Sonatenform bei Brahms* (Vienna, 1927), p 250.

242 Christian Martin Schmidt, *Motivisch-thematische Vermittlung in der Musik von Johannes Brahms* (Munich, 1971), p 184.

243 Arnold Schoenberg, *Style and Idea: Selected Writings*, ed Leonard Stein (London, 1975), pp 398–441.

244 Stahmer, p 196.

245 Brahms to Fritz Simrock (21 Dec 1876), *Briefwechsel*, vol 10, pp 20f.

246 Sturke

247 Gál, p 203.

248 Kalbeck, vol 1, p 165.

249 Litzmann, vol 2, p 209.

250 Brahms to Joachim (Vienna, Sep 1862), *L&L*, p 250.

251 Ibid.

252 Brahms to Clara Schumann (Hamburg, 27 Jan 1860), *L&L*, p 212.

253 Siegmund Helms, *Die Melodienbildung in den Liedern von Johannes Brahms und ihr Verhältnis zu Volksliedern und volkstümlichen Weisen*, dissertation, Berlin, 1968.

254 Brahms to Joachim (14 Oct 1894), *Briefwechsel*, vol 6, p 292.

255 Brahms to Clara Schumann, *CS-JB*, vol 2, p 261.

256 Gál, p 186

257 Ecclesiastes, 4:2.

258 Richard Wagner, *Gesammelte Schriften und Dichtungen,* Berlin, 1914.

259 Gál, p 193 and *L&L*, p 429 both refer.

260 Brahms to Clara Schumann (1888), *CS-JB Briefe*, vol 2, p 322.

261 Brahms to Karl Reinecke (Vienna, Dec 1876), *L&L*, p 505.

262 Theodor Billroth to Hanslick (15 Dec 1876), *Brahms und Billroth*, p 228, fn.

263 Brahms to Joachim (Vienna, 21 Jan 1879), *Briefwechsel*, vol 6, p 153.

264 Brahms to Elisabet von Herzogenberg (Vienna, Jan 1879), *Herzogenberg*, p 77.

265 Brahms to Joachim (Leipzig,

28 Jan 1859), *L&L*, p 189.

266 Brahms to Clara Schumann (1888), *CS-JB Briefe*, vol 2, p 322.

267 Brahms to Emma Engelmann (Preßbaum, 7 Jul 1881), *L&L*, p 580.

268 Botstein, p 73.

269 Brahms to Joachim (Thun, 24 Jul 1887), *L&L*, p 647.

270 Walter Rehberg, Paula Rehberg, *Johannes Brahms. Sein Leben und sein Werk* (Zurich, 2nd ed 1963), p 355.

271 Arnold Schoenberg, 'Kriterien zur Bewertung von Musik', quoted in Dümling, p 50.

272 Arnold Schoenberg to Alfred V Frankenstein (Los Angeles, 18 Mar 1939), Arnold Schoenberg, *Letters*, sel and ed Erwin Stein (London, 1964), pp 207–8; the occasional slightly odd English is Schoenberg's own.

273 Stahmer, p 167.

274 Botstein, p 129.

275 Brahms to Clara Schumann (Ischl, July 1891), *CS-JB*, vol 2, p 196.

276 Carl Dahlhaus, 'Brahms und die Idee der Kammermusik', in Dümling, p 59.

277 Brahms to Clara Schumann (Switzerland, Sep 1868), *L&L*, p 366; *CS-JB*, vol 2, p 229.

Chronology

Year	Age	Life
1833		7 May, born in Hamburg.
1840	7	Piano lessons from Otto Friedrich Willibald Cossel; Played with his father in taverns.
1843	10	First public appearance as pianist; a tour of America proposed for the 'child prodigy', which Cossel prevents; Brahms sent to a famous teacher, Eduard Marxsen.
1848/49	15/16	First concerts; plays one of his own pieces, Fantasy on a Well-loved Waltz, for the first time.
1853	20	Tour with Ede Reményi; meets the violinist Joseph Joachim in Hanover, Liszt in Weimar and Robert and Clara Schumann in Düsseldorf. Schumann writes his essay, 'New Paths', announcing the arrival of a new musical genius.
1854	21	Robert Schumann throws himself off a bridge into the Rhine and is taken to the clinic in Endenich. Brahms's affection for Clara Schumann develops into a passion.
1855	22	Journey along the Rhine with Clara Schumann; concert tour.

Year	History	Culture
1833	In British Empire, slavery abolished. Michael Faraday discovers electrolysis.	Felix Mendelssohn, Fourth Symphony.
1840	In New Zealand, Treaty of Waitangi: Maori chiefs surrender sovereignty to Britain. In Canada, Act of Union joins Lower and Upper Canada. In south Africa, Ndebele found Matabeleland.	Robert Schumann, *Dichterliebe*. Adolphe Sax invents the saxophone. P J Proudhon, *Qu'est-ce-que la propriété?*
1843	In India, Britain annexes Sind. In south Africa, Britain proclaims Natal a colony.	Gaetano Donizetti, *Don Pasquale*. Richard Wagner, *Flying Dutchman*. Charles Dickens, *A Christmas Carol*. John Stuart Mill, *Logic*. In Britain, the *Economist* magazine founded. J M W Turner, *The Sun of Venice Going to Sea*. John Ruskin, *Modern Painters* (until 1860).
1848	In continental Europe, revolutions in: Sicily; Naples; Paris; Vienna; Venice; Milan; Warsaw; and Cracow. In France, Second Republic begins (until 1851). In French West Indies, slavery abolished. Treaty of Guadeloupe: US authority over western and southwestern states. In India, second Sikh War	1848 Elizabeth Gaskell, *Mary Barton*. William Thackeray, *Vanity Fair*. Friedrich Engels and Karl Marx, *The Communist Manifesto*. Mill, *Principles of Political Economy*. H Holman Hunt, J Millais and D G Rossetti form the Pre-Raphaelite Brotherhood.
1853	In Rome, republic proclaimed; French troops take Rome. In India, Britain annexes Punjab.	Giuseppe Verdi, *Il Trovatore* and *La Traviata*.
1854	In US, Republican Party founded. Pope Piux X declares the dogma of Immaculate Conception of Blessed Virgin Mary to be an article of faith.	Hector Berlioz, *L'enfance du Christ*.
1855	In Russia, Nicholas I dies; Alexander II becomes tsar. In southern Africa, David Livingstone 'discovers' Victoria Falls.	Robert Browning, *Men and Women*. Gaskell, *North and South*. Walt Whitman, *Leaves of Grass*.

1856	23	27 July: Robert Schumann dies. Brahms separates from Clara Schumann.
1857	24	Brahms in Detmold; first experience of conducting a choir.
1858	25	Meets Agathe von Siebold in Göttingen; they get engaged, but Brahms withdraws.
1859	26	In Detmold again; during the autumn the two Serenades, Op 11 and Op 16, are written. After a long genesis, the First Piano Concerto Op 15 is completed; it is a flop in Leipzig.
1860	27	Manifesto directed against the 'New German School' centred on Liszt.
1861	28	Living in the Hamburg suburb of Hamm; writes the Handel Variations Op 24.
1862	29	First visit to Vienna. The direction of the Philharmonic Society in Hamburg, which Brahms had hoped for, is given to the singer, Julius Stockhausen.
1863	30	Writes *Rinaldo* Op 50 in Blankenese. Offered the direction of the Vienna *Singakademie*, which he accepts.
1864	31	Resigns as choirmaster of the *Singakademie*.

1856	Treaty of Paris: integrity of Turkey is recognized. Second Anglo-Chinese war. Henry Bessemer discovers process of converting iron into steel.	Liszt, *Hungarian Rhapsodies* Robert Schumann dies
1857	In India, mutiny against the British. In Africa, J H Speke 'discovers' source of the Nile. Laying of cable under Atlantic Ocean begins.	Charles Baudelaire, *Les Fleurs du Mal*. Gustave Flaubert, *Madame Bovary*. Anthony Trollope, *Barchester Towers*. J F Millet, *The Gleaners*. Jacques Offenbach, *Orpheus in the Underworld*.
1858	Dissolution of English East India Company. At Lourdes, apparition of Virgin Mary.	George Eliot, *Adam Bede*.
1859	Franco-Piedmontese War against Austria. Spanish-Moroccan War. Construction of Suez Canal begins.	C F Gounod, *Faust*. Wagner, *Tristan und Isolde*. Edward Fitzgerald, *Rubaiyat of Omar Khayyam*. Charles Darwin, *The Origin of Species by Natural Selection*. Mill, *On Liberty*. Edouard Manet, *Absinthe Drinker*.
1860	In Italy, unification achieved by invasions of Garibaldi and Victor Emmanuel respectively. In New Zealand, Taranaki wars.	George Eliot, *The Mill on the Floss*. Ivan Turgenev, *On the Eve*. J Burckhardt, *The Culture of the Renaissance in Italy*.
1861	In US, Abraham Lincoln becomes president. In US, Civil War begins. In Italy, Victor Emmanuel II becomes king. In Russia, serfdom abolished. In Britain, death of Prince Albert.	Dickens, *Great Expectations*. Eliot, *Silas Marner*.
1862	In Prussia, Otto von Bismarck becomes premier.	Verdi, *La Forza del Destino*. Victor Hugo, *Les misérables*. Turgenev, *Fathers and Sons*.
1863	In US, slavery abolished. In Asia, Cambodia becomes French protectorate. Polish uprising against Russia.	Berlioz, *The Trojans* (part I). Charles Kingsley, *The Water Babies*. Ernest Renan, *La Vie de Jésus*. Manet, *Déjeuner sur l'herbe*.
1864	In London, Karl Marx organizes First Socialist International. British, French and Dutch fleets attack	Anton Bruckner, Mass No 1 in D minor.

1865	32	Death of his mother; composes his *German Requiem* Op 45.
1866	33	His father marries again; Brahms immediately has a good relationship with his stepmother, whom he later provides for
1868	35	First performance of the *German Requiem* in Bremen; the *Hungarian Dances* are published.
1869	36	The *Magelone Romanzen*, begun in 1861, are completed.
1870	37	First performance of Alto Rhapsody, Op 53.
1871	38	Inspired by the German victory over France, Brahms writes the *Triumphlied* Op 55; it is performed immediately, in April in Bremen and in June in Karlsruhe.
1872	39	Brahms appointed director of the Vienna *Singverein*; moves to 4 Karlsgasse; his father dies.
1873	40	Completes the Haydn Variations Op 56 during his summer stay in Tutzing.
1874	41	Spends the summer in Rüschlikon near Zurich; renewal of his friendship with Elisabet and Heinrich Herzogenberg in Leipzig.
1875	42	Resigns directorship of Vienna *Singverein*.

	Japanese in Shimonoseki Straits. Henri Dunant founds Red Cross. Louis Pasteur invents pasteurization.	
1865	In US, Abraham Lincoln assassinated. In Belgium, Leopold I dies; Leopold II becomes king. In South America, Paraguayan war. End of transport of convicts to Australia.	Lewis Carroll, *Alice's Adventures in Wonderland*.
1866	Austro-Prussian War. Austro-Italian War. In Canada, Fenian 'invasion'. Alfred Nobel invents dynamite. Gregor Mendel develops laws of heredity.	Friedrich Smetana, *The Bartered Bride*. Fyodor Dostoyevsky, *Crime and Punishment*.
1868	In Britain, William Gladstone becomes prime minister. In Japan, Meiji dynasty restored. In Britain, Trades' Union Congress founded.	Wilkie Collins, *The Moonstone*.
1869	Suez Canal opens.	Wagner, *The Rhinegold*.
1870	Franco-Prussian War	
1871	At Versailles, Wilhelm proclaimed German emperor. In France, Third Republic suppresses Paris Commune and loses Alsace- Lorraine to Germany. In Africa, H M Stanley finds D Livingstone at Ujiji.	Verdi, *Aïda*.
1872	In Philippines, rebellion against Spain. First International Association Football match, England versus Scotland.	Thomas Hardy, *Under the Greenwood Tree*.
1873	In Spain, Amadeo I abdicates; republic proclaimed. In Africa, Ashanti War begins. In Asia, Acheh War.	Arthur Rimbaud, *A Season in Hell*. Walter Pater, *Studies in the History of the Renaissance*. Claude Monet, *Impression: soleil levant*.
1874	In Britain, Benjamin Disraeli becomes prime minister. In Spain, Alfonso XII establishes con- stitutional monarchy. Britain annexes Fiji islands.	Smetana, *My Fatherland*. J Strauss, *Die Fledermaus*. In Paris, First Impressionist Exhibition.
1875	In China, Kwang-Su becomes emperor Russo-Japanese agreement over Sakhalin and the Kuriles. In Bosnia and Herzegovina, revolts against Turkish rule.	Tchaikovsky, First Piano Concerto in B flat minor. Georges Bizet, *Carmen*. Mark Twain, *The Adventures of Tom Sawyer*. Monet, *Boating at Argenteuil*.

1876	43	The First Symphony in C minor Op 68 completed; first performance on 4 December under Otto Dessoff in Karlsruhe.
1877	44	First summer in Pörtschach; works on his Second Symphony in D major Op 73; first performance on 30 December under Hans Richter in Vienna.
1878	45	Second summer in Pörtschach; composes the Violin Concerto in D major Op 77; first trip to Italy with Theodor Billroth.
1879	46	Honorary doctorate from University of Breslau; third and last summer in Pörtschach; concert tour with Joachim to Transylvania.
1880	47	Summer in Bad Ischl; writes the two Overtures Op 80 and Op 81, of which he says *One is laughing, the other crying.*
1881	48	Completes his Second Piano Concerto Op 83 in Pressbaum outside Vienna and plays it from his manuscript score in Budapest. Bülow performs it in several German cities with his exemplary Meiningen orchestra.
1883	50	Summer in Wiesbaden; completes his Third Symphony in F major Op 90; first performance in Vienna in December under Hans Richter.
1884	51	Visits the Duchy of Meiningen; summer in Mürzzuschlag, Styria; begins the Fourth Symphony in E minor Op 98.
1885	52	Second summer in Mürzzuschlag; completes his Fourth Symphony, which has its first performance on 25 October in Meiningen.

1876	China declares Korea an independent state.	Wagner, *Siegfried*. First complete performance of Wagner's *The Ring*.
	Turkish massacre of Bulgarians.	
	Battle of Little Bighorn; General Custer dies.	
	Alexander Graham Bell invents telephone.	
1877	Russo-Turkish War.	Emile Zola, *L'Assommoir*.
	Britain annexes Transvaal.	
	Porfirio Diaz becomes president of Mexico.	
	In Japan, Satsuma rebellion suppressed.	
	Thomas Edison invents gramophone.	
	In Britain, first Wimbledon tennis tournament.	
1878	Congress of Berlin resolves Balkan crisis.	Tchaikovsky, *Eugene Onegin*.
	Serbia becomes independent.	
	Britain gains Cyprus.	
	Second Anglo-Afghan War.	
	In London, electric street lighting.	
1879	Germany and Austria-Hungary form Dual Alliance.	Bruckner, Sixth Symphony. Henrik Ibsen, *The Doll's House*. August Strindberg, *The Red Room*.
	In Africa, Zulu War.	
	In south Africa, Boers proclaim Transvaal Republic.	
	In South America, War of the Pacific.	
1880	First Boer War.	Tchaikovsky, *1812 Overture*. Dostoyevsky, *The Brothers Karamazov*.
	Louis Pasteur discovers streptococcus.	
1881	In Russia, Alexander II assassinated.	Jacques Offenbach, *The Tales of Hoffmann*.
	In Japan, political parties established.	Anatole France, *Le Crime de Sylvestre Bonnard*.
	Tunisia becomes French protectorate.	
	In Algeria, revolt against the French.	Henry James, *Portrait of a Lady*.
	In Sudan, Mahdi Holy War.	Ibsen, *Ghosts*.
	In eastern Europe, Jewish pogroms.	
1883	Jewish immigration to Palestine (Rothschild Colonies).	Robert Louis Stevenson, *Treasure Island*.
	Germany acquires southwest Africa.	
	In Chicago, world's first skyscraper built.	
1884	Sino-French War.	Jules Massenet, *Manon*.
	Berlin Conference to mediate European claims in Africa.	Twain, *Huckleberry Finn*. Georges Seurat, *Une Baignade, Asnières*.
	In Mexico, Porfirio Diaz becomes president.	
1885	Belgium's King Leopold II establishes Independent Congo State.	Zola, *Germinal*. Guy de Maupassant, *Bel Ami*.
	In Transvaal, gold discovered.	
	Gottlieb Daimler invents prototype of motorcycle.	

1886	53	Brahms made honorary president of the Vienna *Tonkünstlerverein*; spends the summer, and the two following, in Hofstätten on Lake Thun. There he writes the Cello Sonata Op 99, the two Violin Sonatas Op 100 and Op 108 and the Double Concerto for Violin and Cello in A minor Op 102.
1889	56	Made freeman of the city of Hamburg; spends the summer in Ischl, where in 1890 he completes the String Quintet in G major Op 111, in 1891 the Clarinet Trio in A minor Op 114 and in 1892 the Clarinet Quintet in B minor Op 115.
1893	60	Last trip to Italy and last summer in Ischl.
1895	62	Brahms Festival in Meiningen; other cities follow suit. Clarinet Sonatas, Op 120.
1896	63	20 May: death of Clara Schumann. Brahms completes *Four Serious Songs* Op 121.
1897	64	Brahms dies on 3 April and is buried in the *Zentralfriedhof* (the Central Cemetery) in Vienna.

1886	In Cuba, slavery abolished. In India, first meeting of National Congress. In Canada, Canadian Pacific Railway completed.	H Rider Haggard, *King Solomon's Mines*. Stevenson, *Dr Jekyll and Mr Hyde*. Rimbaud, *Les Illuminations*. Leo Tolstoy, *The Death of Ivan Ilich*.
1889	Second Socialist International. Italy invades Somalia and Ethiopia. In Paris, Eiffel Tower completed. Brazil proclaims itself a republic.	Richard Strauss, *Don Juan*. Verdi, *Falstaff*. George Bernard Shaw, *Fabian Essays*.
1893	Franco-Russian alliance signed. British South Africa Company launches Matabele War. France annexes Laos.	Dvořák, *New World Symphony*. Tchaikovsky, *Pathétique*. Oscar Wilde, *A Woman of No Importance*.
1895	In Britain, Lord Salisbury becomes prime minister. Cuban rebellion begins. Japan conquers Formosa (Taiwan). Lumière brothers invent the cinematograph. Guglielmo Marconi invents wireless telegraphy. Wilhelm Röntgen discovers X-rays.	H G Wells, *The Time Machine*. W B Yeats, *Poems*. Wilde, *The Importance of Being Earnest*.
1896	Theodor Herzl founds Zionism. First Olympic Games of the modern era held in Athens. Antoine (Henri) Becquerel discovers radioactivity of uranium.	Giacomo Puccini, *La Bohème*. Thomas Hardy, *Jude the Obscure*.
1897	In Britain, Queen Victoria celebrates Diamond Jubilee. British destroy Benin City. Klondike gold rush. J J Thomson discovers electron.	Joseph Conrad, *The Nigger of the Narcissus*. Stefan George, *Das Jahr der Seele*. Strindberg, *Inferno*. Edmond Rostand, *Cyrano de Bergerac*.

List of Works

(The year in brackets refers to the date of first publication.)

ORCHESTRAL WORKS

Symphony, c minor, Op 68 (1862–76)
Symphony, D major, Op 73 (1877)
Symphony, F major, Op 90 (1883)
Symphony, e minor, Op 98 (1884–5)
Serenade, No 1 D major, Op 11 (1857–60)
Serenade No 2, A major, Op 16 (1858–60)
Variation on a theme by Joseph Haydn, Op 56 (1873)
Academic Festival Overture, Op 80 (1880)
Tragic Overture, Op 81 (1880)
Hungarian Dances (editions, 1874 and 1881)

CONCERTOS

First Piano Concerto, d minor, Op 15 (1854–58)
Second Piano Concerto, B flat major, Op 83 (1878-81)
Violin Concerto, D major, Op 77 (1878)
Double Concerto for violin and cello, a-minor, Op 102 (1887)

CHAMBER MUSIC

With piano:

Quintet in F minor, Op 34 (1861–4)
Quartet No 1, g minor, Op 25 (1861)
Quartet No 2, A major, Op 26 (1861)
Quartet No 3, c minor, Op 60 (1855–75)
Trio in B major, Op 8 (1854, new version 1889)
Trio in E flat-major, for the piano, violin and horn, Op 40 (1865)

Trio in C major, Op 87 (188–82)
Trio in c minor, Op 101 (1886)
Trio in a minor for the piano, clarinet and cello, Op 114 (1891)
Sonata No 1, G major, for piano and violin, Op 78 (1878–9)
Sonata No 2, A major, for piano and violin, Op 100 (1886)
Sonata No 3, d minor, for piano and violin, Op 108 (1886–8)
Scherzo for violin and piano Wo 02 (1853)
Sonata No 1, e minor, for piano and cello, Op 38 (1862–65)
Sonata No 2, F major, for piano and cello, Op 99 (1886)
2 sonatas for piano and clarinet, Op 120 (1895)
No 1 in f minor
No 2 in E flat major

Without piano:

String Sextet No 2, G major, Op 36 (1864–5)
String Quintet No 1, F major, Op 88 (1882)
String Quintet No 2, (1890)
Clarinet Quintet b-minor, op 115 (1891)
String Quartet No 1, c minor, Op 51/1 (1863-75)
String Quartet No 2, a minor, Op 51/2 (1863–75)
String Quartet No 3, B flat major, Op 67 (1875)

PIANO MUSIC

For two hands:

Sonata No 1 in C major, Op 1 (1852–3)
Sonata No 2 in f sharp-minor, Op 2 (1852)
Sonata No 3 in f minor, Op 5 (1853)
Scherzo in f flat minor, Op 4 (1851)
Variations on a theme by Schumann, Op 9 (1854)
Variations on an original theme, Op 21/1 (1857)
Variation on a Hungarian Song, Op 21/ 2 (1856)
Variations and fugue on a theme by Handel, Op 24 (1861)
Variations on a theme by Paganini, Op 35 (1862–3)
4 ballades, Op 10 (1854)
8 piano pieces, Op 76 (1878)

2 Rhapsodies, Op 79 (1879)
7 Fantasia, Op 116 (1892)
3 Intermezzi, Op 117 (1892)
6 Piano Pieces, Op 118 (1892)
4 Piano Pieces, Op 119 (1893)
Hungarian dances (1872, edition of four-handed originals)

For four hands:

Variations on a theme by Schumann, Op 23 (1861)
Waltzes, Op 39 (1865)
Hungarian dances, four books Wo 07 (1869)

ORGAN MUSIC

Fugue in a Flat-minor (1864)
Choral prelude and fugue on *O Traurigkeit, o Herzeleid* (1882)
11 Choral preludes, Op 122 (1896)

CHORUS AND ORCHESTRA

For Mixed Chorus:

A German requiem, Op 45 (1857-68)
Schicksalslied, Op 54 (1868–71)
Triumphlied, Op 55 (1870–1)
Naenie, Op 82 (1880–1)
Gesäng der Parzen, Op 89 (1882)
Begr bnisgesang, Op 13 (1858)

For female chorus:

Ave Maria, Op 12 (1858)

For male chorus:

Rinaldo, cantata for tenor, male chorus and orchestra, Op 50 (1863–8)
Rhapsody for Alto Male Chorus and orchestra, Op 53 (1869)

POLYPHONIC VOCAL MUSIC WITHOUT ORCHESTRA

For mixed voices with accompaniment:

Geistliches Lieder, Op 30, with organ and piano (1856)

3 Vocal quartets with piano, Op 31 (1859–63)

3 Vocal quartets with piano, Op 64 (1862–74)

4 Vocal quartets with piano, Op 92 (1877–84)

6 Vocal quartets with piano, Op 112 (1888–91)

Liebeslieder, waltzes, with four-handed piano, Op 62 and Op 65 (1869–74)

Zigeunerlieder, with piano, Op 103 (1887)

Tafellied, Op 93b (1884)

For mixed voices a cappella:

Marienlieder, Op 22 (1859)

2 Motets, Op 29 (1859)

2 Motets, Op 74 (1859–77)

3 Motets, Op 110 (1889)

Fest-und Gedenksprüche, Op 109 (1888-9)

3 *Gesänge*, Op 42 (1859–61)

7 *Lieder*, Op 62 (1860–74)

7 Songs and Romances, Op 93a (1883–4)

5 *Gesänge*, Op 104 (1886–88)

14 German folk songs (1864)

12 German folk songs Wo 035, (1927) Canons etc (Op posth. 1927)

For female voices with accompaniment:

Psalm 13, Op 27 with organ or piano (1859)

4 *Gesänge* with two horns and harp, Op 17 (1860)

For female voices a cappella:

3 Sacred choruses, Op 37 (1859–63)

12 Songs and Romances, Op 44 (1859–61)

13 Canons, Op 113 (1860–67)

For male voices a cappella:

5 *Lieder*, Op 41 (1861–2)

SONGS FOR ONE SINGING VOICE WITH PIANO ACCOMPANIMENT

6 *Gesänge*, Op 3 (1851)
6 *Gesänge*, Op 6 (1852–3)
6 *Gesänge*, Op 7 (1851–3)
8 *Lieder und Romanzen*, Op 14 (1858)
5 poems, Op 19 (1852)
8 *Lieder and Gesänge*, Op 32 (1864)
15 romances from Tieck's 'Magelone Romanzen', Op 33 (1865–69)
4 *Gesänge*, Op 43 (1868)
4 *Lieder*, Op 46 (1868)
5 *Lieder*, Op 47 (1868)
7 *Lieder*, Op 48 (1868)
5 *Lieder*, Op 49 (1868)
8 *Lieder and Gesänge*, Op 57 (1871)
8 *Lieder and Gesänge*, Op 58 (1871)
8 *Lieder and Gesänge*, Op 59 (1873)
9 *Lieder and Gesänge*, Op 63 (1874)
9 *Gesänge*, Op 69 (1877)
4 *Gesänge*, Op 70 (1877)
5 *Gesänge*, Op 71 (1877)
5 *Gesänge*, Op 72 (1877)
5 romances and *Lieder* for one or two vocal voices, Op 84 (1882)
6 *Lieder*, Op 85 (1882)
6 *Lieder* Op 86 (1882)
2 *Gesänge* for alto and viola and piano, Op 91 (1884)
5 *Lieder* for a low voice, Op 94 (1884)
7 *Lieder*, Op 95 (1884)
4 *Lieder*, Op 96 (1885)
6 *Lieder*, Op 97 (1886)
5 *Lieder* for a lower voice, Op 105 (1889)
5 *Lieder*, Op 106 (1889)
5 *Lieder*, Op 107 (1889)
4 Serious Songs *Gesänge* for a bass voice, Op 121 (1896)
28 folk songs (Op posth. 1858)

14 Children Songs Wo O 31 (1858)

DUETS FOR TWO VOICES WITH PIANO

3 Duets for soprano and alto, Op 20 (1858–60)
4 Duets for alto and baritone, Op 28 (1860–62)
4 Duets for soprano and alto, Op 61 (1852–74)
5 Duets for soprano and alto, Op 66 (1875)
4 Ballads and romances for two voices, Op 75 (1877–8)

Select Discography

Symphonies Nos 1–4
Berlin Philharmonic Orchestra/ Herbert von Karajan (cond)
Deutsche Grammophon   474 263-2 (2 CD)

Vienna Philharmonic Orchestra and Berlin Philharmonic Orchestra/
Wilhelm Furtwängler (cond) *Mono; historic recordings from the years
1948–1956.*
EMI Références 7243 5 65513 2 9 (3 CD)

Piano Concertos Nos 1 & 2
Stephen Kovacevich (pf)/ London Philharmonic Orchestra/ Wolfgang
Sawallisch (cond)
EMI / Double Forte 7243 5 75655 2 (2 CD)

Emil Gilels (pf)/ Berlin Philharmonic Orchestra/ Eugen Jochum
(cond)
Deutsche Grammophon   447 446-2 (2 CD)

Piano Concerto No 2
Vladimir Horowitz (pf) NBC Symphony Orchestra/ Arturo Toscanini
(cond) *Historic mono recording from the year 1940. Rehearsal of Brahms'
1ˢᵗ Symphony included.*
Naxos/ Historical 8.110805-6 (2 CD)

Violin Concerto
Kyung-Wha Chung (vn)/ Vienna Philharmonic Orchestra/ Simon
Rattle (cond)
EMI 7243 5 57165-2.

Fritz Kreisler (vn)/ London Philharmonic Orchestra/ John Barbirolli
(cond). *Mono; historic recording from the year 1924.*
Naxos/ Historical 8.110843

Double Concerto Op 102
Gidon Kremer (vn), Clemens Hagen (vc)/ Royal Concertgebouw
Orchestra/ Nikolaus Harnoncourt (cond)
Teldec (Warner Music) 0630-13137-2

Violin Sonatas Nos 1–3
Henryk Szerying (vn), Arthur Rubinstein (pf)
RCA/ Red Seal 09026 63041-2

Cello Sonatas Nos 1 & 2
Heinrich Schiff (vc), Gerhard Oppitz (pf)
Philips 456 402-2

Clarinet Sonatas Nos 1 & 2
Gervase de Peyer (cl), Gwenneth Pryor (pf)
Chandos CHAN 8563

Complete Trios
Beaux Arts Trio, Francis Orval (hn), George Pieterson (clar), György
Sebok (pf), Arthur Grumiaux (vn)
Philips 438 603-2 (2 CD)

Piano Quartets Nos 1-3
Isaac Stern (vn), Jaime Laredo (va), Yo-Yo Ma (vc), Emanuel Ax (pf)
Sony Classical S2K 45846 (2 CD)

Piano Quintet
Quartetto Italiano & Maurizio Pollini (pf)
Deutsche Grammophon 419 673-2

String Quartets Nos 1-3
Alban Berg Quartet
EMI 0777 7 54829 2 (2 CD)

String Quintets Nos 1 & 2
Hagen Quartet & Gérard Caussée (va)
Deutsche Grammophon 453 420-2

String Sextets Nos 1 & 2
Academy of St Martin in the Fields Chamber Ensemble
Chandos   CHAN 9151

Piano Solo *(various)*
Intermezzi/ Variations on a Theme by Paganini/ Sonata No 3 etc.
Julius Katchen (pf)
Decca/ Double Decca 452 338

Wilhelm Kempff (pf) *(partly mono)*
Philips/ Great Pianists of the 20th Century 456 862-2

Lieder *(various)* **/ Vier ernste Gesänge**
Dietrich Fischer-Dieskau (bar) & Jörg Demus (pf)
Deutsche Grammophon 463 509-2

49 Deutsche Volkslieder (*49 German Folksongs***)**
Stephan Genz (bar), Roger Vignoles (pf)
Teldec (Warner Music) 3984-23700-2.

Ein deutsches Requiem *(German Requiem)*
Charlotte Margione (sop), Rodney Gilfry (bar)/Orchestre
Révolutionnaire et Romantique & Monteverdi Choir/John Eliot
Gardiner (cond)
Philips 432 140-2

Picture Sources

Photo Research by Image Select International Ltd. 2 Marston Court, Cromwell, Business Park, Chipping Norton, Oxfordshire. OX7 5SR United Kingdom.

Grateful thanks are extended by the publisher to the Lecbrecht Collection, Topfoto Picture Agency and ARPL (Anne Ronan Picture Library) for their pictures, supplied for this book.

ARPL: Title page, Prelim page iii; Prelim page vi; Prelim page vii, Prelim page xii, Page 10, Page 17 left and right, Page 20, Page 29, Page 76, Page 78, Page 81, Page 82, Page 105, Page 106, Page 108, Page 109, Page 112, Page 133.

Lebrecht Collection: Page 6, Page 7, Page 25, Page 34, Page 38, Page 39, Page 44, Page 50, Page 57, Page 65, Page 73, Page 84, Page 92, Page 95, Page 99, Page 100, Page 103, Page 110, Page 119, Page 126, Page 130.

Topfoto: Page 143.

Index

Ahsen, Fräulein Jenny von, 62
Aichholz, Victor von Miller zu, 117
Allgemeine Musikalische Zeitung, 19, 24
Allgeyer, Julius, 98–9, 100
Alsace, 9
Amati, Andrea, 32
America, 18, 25, 26
atonality, 143

Bach, C P E, 140
Bach, Johann Sebastian, 96, 125; portrait
    of, 11; influence on Brahms, 69–70,
    76, 77, 79, 121, 132; revival, 80;
    Cantor of Leipzig Thomaskirche, 103,
    106; 'Chaconne', 138; *Goldberg*
    Variations, 70; *Liebster Gott, wann werd*
    ich sterben, 82; Toccata in F major, 51,
    72
Bad Ischl, 98, 99, 105, 106, 121, 143
Baden-Baden, 76, 77, 98, 99
Bargheer, Carl, 53
Bayreuth, 4, 8–9, 114, 143
Beckerath, Willy von, vii–viii, xi, 76
Beethoven, Ludwig van, ix, 5, 54, 67,
    72, 75, 96, 134, 137, 140; manu-
    scripts, ix, 50, 79; Brahms as 'heir',
    3, 72, 121; statue of, 11; influence
    on Brahms, 69, 114, 128; love of
    nature, 98; 'Hammerklavier', 50;
    Kreutzer Sonata, 24; *Lieder*, 64;
    Ninth Symphony, 54, 122; Ruins of
    Athens, 56
Berg, Alban, 3
Berlin, 1; Sternscher Gesangverein, 65
Berliner Tageblatt, 92
Bible, 8, 133
Billroth, Theodor, 96–7, 102, 135–6;
    biography, 97
Bismarck, Otto von, 11, 133
Blankenese, 75

Blaue Reiter, 3
Boccaccio, Giovanni, 11
Böcklin, Arnold, 11
Böhm, Joachim, 25
Brahms, Elise, 52
Brahms, Johann Jakob, 15–16, 17
Brahms, Johanna Henrika Christina (née
    Nissen), 17
Brahms, Johannes: self-image, viii; com-
    positional method, ix–xi; manu-
    scripts, ix–xi, 24, 37–8, 105;
    self-doubt, 2, 6; musical influences,
    2–3, 6, 50, 69–70, 80–81, 121–2;
    'Beethoven's heir', 3, 72, 121; com-
    positional technique, 3; his influence,
    3–4, 126; love of books, 4, 10–11;
    apolitical, 7, 9; patriotism, 7–9;
    Romanticism, 10, 23–4, 33, 120; his
    will, 11, 24, 107; financial security,
    12, 70–71, 88–9; failure to marry,
    13, 60–61, 101; birth, 17; musical
    apprenticeship, 18; shyness, 20, 28,
    85; reticence, 21, 54, 83–6, 126,
    143; friendships, 21, 65, 85, 96,
    98–9; friendship with Reményi,
    24–5; friendship with Joachim,
    25–32, 93, 139; early compositions,
    25, 36, 37; *Hungarian Dances* scandal,
    26, 86–7; dispute with New
    Germans, 28, 37, 67, 110–11;
    walking tour of Rhineland, 32–3;
    Schumann's 'New Paths' article,
    34–7, 109, 111, 127, 140; gravity,
    38; meets Clara Schumann, 39; rela-
    tionship with Clara Schumann, 41–9,
    84, 135, 141; 'Werther experience',
    48, 60, 128; reputation as pianist,
    49; renunciation of Clara Schumann,
    24, 52, 59–61, 88; walking, 53; pre-
    occupation with form, 55; relation-

ship with Agathe von Siebold, 58–61, 88; 'Agathe summer', 59, 60, 67; later friendship with Clara Schumann, 60, 63–4; 'Hamburg years', 62–9; leaves Hamburg, 71, 75, 88; first visit to Vienna, 71–5; as conductor, 76; settled in Vienna, 76, 78, 83, 88, 128; Florence May's pen portrait, 77–8; as teacher, 77–8; work on earlier composers, 78–80; relationship with Elisabet von Herzogenberg, 83–6; strength of character, 87; collaboration with Bülow, 90–94; appearance, 95–6; friendship with Billroth, 96–7; love of nature, 98; failure to write opera, 99–101; relationship with Hermine Spies, 102; Christianity, 105; fear of death, 105; final illness and death, 106–8; attitude to Wagner, 111–14, 115; attitude to contemporaries, 114–19; Central German Romantic School, 121

COMPOSITIONS: C major Sonata Op 1, 52, 129, 132, 139; Sonata for Piano in F sharp minor Op 2, 39, 52, 139; *Gesänge* Op 3, 131; Scherzo in E flat minor Op 4, 27, 51, 139; Piano Sonata in F minor Op 5, 33, 139, 140; B major Piano Trio Op 8, 141; First Serenade Op 11, 54, 58, 66, 136; *Ave Maria* Op 12, 62, 66; *Begräbnisgesang* Op 13, 66; *Lieder und Romanzen* Op 14, 66; First Piano Concerto Op 15, 55–7, 65, 85, 119, 135, 137; Second Serenade Op 16, 58, 65, 66; B flat String Sextet Op 18, 65; *Marienlieder* Op 22, 131; Variations on a Theme by Schumann Op 23, 69; Variations and Fugue on a Theme by Handel Op 24, 69–70, 72, 111; G minor Piano Quartet Op 25, 68, 71, 72, 141; Piano Quartet in A major Op 26, 72; motet Op 29, 131; *Lieder und Gesänge* Op 32, 84; *Magelone Romanzen* Op 33, 64–5,

131; *Paganini Variations* Op 35, 74, 75; G major String Sextet Op 36, 61; *12 Songs and Romances* Op 44, 60; *A German Requiem* Op 45, 85, 88, 127, 128, 132, 134; *Rinaldo* Op 50, 75; A minor String Quartet Op 51, 96; *Liebeslieder Waltzer* Op 52, 130; *Alto Rhapsody* Op 53, 101, 131; *Schicksalslied* Op 54, 103, 133; *Triumphlied* Op 55, 7–8, 133; *Haydn Variations* Op 56, 128; C minor Piano Quartet Op 60, 48, 86, 126, 128; *Liebeslieder Waltzer* Op 65, 130; B flat major String Quartet Op 67, 83, 86, 142; First Symphony Op 68, 2, 86, 122, 126, 128, 135–6; Second Symphony ('Pastoral') Op 73, 86, 136, 138; motet Op 74, 131; Violin Concerto Op 77, x, 136; G major Op 78 (*Regenlied*), vii, xi, 140; *Rhapsodies* Op 79, x, xi; Second Piano Concerto Op 83, 93, 127, 135, 137, 138; *Lieder* Op 86, 131; Third Symphony Op 90, 32, 127, 138; *Lieder* Op 96 and 97, 102; Fourth Symphony Op 98, 93, 107, 138, 139; F major Sonata Op 99, 140; Sonata in A major Op 100, 40; Double Concerto Op 102, 134, 139; *Lieder* Op 105, 131; *Fest- und Gedenksprüche* Op 109, 133; motet Op 110, 131; Trio Op 114, 143; Clarinet Quintet Op 115, 142, 143; Clarinet Sonatas Op 120, ix–x, 143; *Four Serious Songs* Op 121, 13, 105, 128, 132, 133; 11 Choral Preludes Op 122, 106; *Hungarian Dances* WoO 1, 26, 86–7, 89; *Children's Songs* WoO 31, 129; 49 German Folk Songs WoO 33, 129, 131

Brahms, Peter Heinrich, 15
Breitkopf & Härtel (publisher), 29, 34, 38, 65–6, 70, 79
Bremen, 88
Brendel, Franz, 37, 109, 110
Brentano, Clemens von, 10